T H E   B O O K   O F

SOUPS

T H E   B O O K   O F

SOUPS

LORNA RHODES

Photography by
JON STEWART
assisted by Kay Small

HPBooks
a division of
PRICE STERN SLOAN
Los Angeles

ANOTHER BEST SELLING VOLUME FROM HPBOOKS

HPBooks
A division of Price Stern Sloan, Inc.
360 North La Cienega Boulevard
Los Angeles, California 90048
9 8 7 6 5 4 3 2 ˙

By arrangement with Salamander Books Ltd., and Merehurst Press, London.

This book was created by Merehurst Limited.
Ferry House, 51-57 Lacy Rd., Putney, London SW151PR
Designer: Roger Daniels
Home Economist: Lorna Rhodes, assisted by Linda Tubby
Photographer: Jon Stewart, assisted by Kay Small
Color separation by Kentscan Limited
Printed in Belgium by Proost International Book Production

CONTENTS

INTRODUCTION

Soup's the most versatile and varied dish on a menu. Soup can be made from every type of food—fruit, vegetables, meat, poultry, fish or game. Soup can be uncooked and cold to provide a refreshing opening to a summer meal, or hot and satisfying to provide a warming start to a winter meal. A soup can be served as an elegant starter, become a snack served in a mug with crusty bread, or it may be so chunky and thick it becomes a meal in itself.

The choice of ingredients can be exotic and unusual and may be expensive, like lobster for a special occasion, but choosing cheap ingredients such as root vegetables or dried beans can result in an equally delicious soup. The combinations of textures, flavors and colors are endless.

There are over 100 exciting soup recipes in this book. Each recipe is illustrated in color and has step-by-step instructions for making the soup, plus different ideas for garnishes and accompaniments.

SOUPS

Soups are ideal for every occasion, and the recipes in this book show just how varied and interesting they can be. Within each chapter there are clear soups, simple puréed soups, soup thickened and enriched with cream and eggs, some flavored with herbs and others with spices. Making soups yourself means that they are nutritious and free from additives, preservatives and colorings. The flavor and texture can suit individual tastes.

The basis of most soups is a well made stock. This is made by simmering meat or bones, a chicken carcass or fish heads and bones with aromatic vegetables and herbs, or just vegetables and herbs, to give a well-flavored liquid. Stock needs to be simmered for a long time, and to be realistic we may not always have the time to make it. If you do, however, it is worthwhile making a large quantity and freezing some. There are excellent stock cubes available to substitute. If too salty, use less of the cube than recommended.

Consommé
It is essential to have a good homemade stock to make consommé, a clear soup made from enriched stock and then clarified to give a crystal clear liquid. Consommé makes an elegant start to any meal.

Broth is also made from stock, but it is not clarified, and the meat or chicken used to make the broth is often served in the soup.

Seasoning
An important rule in soup making is to season toward the end of cooking. Often a liquid reduces during simmering and the soup becomes more concentrated in flavor. Pepper should always be ground into the soup at the last moment to capture its full aromatic and spicy flavor.

Taste after the chilling period and season again, if necessary.

Thickening
There are various ways a soup can be

thickened—puréeing the ingredients reduces the mixture to a smooth consistency. Try varying the texture by not blending the soup until completely smooth.

Alternatively, in some recipes further sieving of the soup may be recommended after puréeing to discard seeds and skins of vegetables or bones of fish.

Using cream and eggs beaten together will enrich a soup and act as a thickener. To prevent curdling, add a little hot soup to the cream mixture before whisking it into the soup.

Freezing

Sometimes, it is difficult to make a small quantity of soup. Cool the extra quickly and then freeze it. Most soups freeze well and it is an excellent way of using excess vegetables or tomatoes.

Avoid adding garlic to a soup which is to be frozen. Also, cream, eggs or milk should not be included before freezing, as these can cause curdling. Add them at the reheating stage.

Use delicate fish soups and oriental soups immediately after preparation or the flavor and texture will deteriorate and reheating will spoil the soup. On the other hand, the robust meat soups, like oxtail, benefit from being refrigerated overnight as the flavors mature and mellow.

Garnishes

A wide range of garnishes can be used to add extra interest to soups, from the simple sprinkling of fresh herbs, grated cheese or swirls of cream, to croutons which can be made in lots of ways with a wide variety of flavorings. Rice and pasta can be used not only as a garnish, but also to make some soups more substantial. The recipes in this book include simple garnishes of cooked and raw vegetables as well as more involved accompaniments such as choux puffs and cheese-filled pastries.

─── CHILLED FISH SOUP ───

1 lb. unpeeled cooked shrimp
3-3/4 cups water
2 strips lemon peel
2 bay leaves
2 blades mace
Salt and pepper to taste
4 small prepared squid, cleaned
Green stems 2 green onions, chopped
4 tomatoes, peeled, seeded, chopped
2 tablespoons peeled chopped cucumber

Peel shrimp and reserve. Place shells, head and tails in a large saucepan. Add water, lemon peel, bay leaves and mace. Season with salt and pepper.

Bring to a boil and simmer 30 minutes. Strain stock through a muslin-lined sieve or coffee filter paper set over a bowl. Return stock to pan. Cut squid in thin rings and chop tentacles. Cook squid in stock 5 minutes and cool.

Stir in reserved shrimp, green onions, tomatoes and cucumber. Season again if necessary. Refrigerate at least 1 hour before serving. Makes 4 servings.

—— SUMMER AVOCADO SOUP ——

2 medium-size ripe avocados
1 tablespoon lemon juice
1 garlic clove, crushed
2/3 cup half and half
2-1/2 cups cold chicken stock
Dash hot-pepper sauce
Salt and pepper to taste
1/2 medium-size avocado and snipped chives to
**   garnish**

Cut 2 avocados in half. Remove seeds and scoop flesh into a food processor fitted with a metal blade or a blender. Add lemon juice, garlic and half and half and process to a puree.

Blend in stock and hot-pepper sauce. Season with salt and pepper.

Pour into a bowl. Cover to prevent discoloration and refrigerate 1 hour. Dice avocado half. Garnish soup with diced avocado and snipped chives. Makes 4 to 6 servings.

CLEAR BEET SOUP

1 onion, coarsely grated
1 large carrot, coarsely grated
1 lb. raw beets, peeled, coarsely grated
Fresh parsley sprig
1 bay leaf
4 cups chicken stock
1 egg white
Juice 1/2 lemon
Salt and pepper to taste
Thin lemon slices to garnish

In a large saucepan, combine vegetables, parsley, bay leaf and stock. Bring to a boil, cover and simmer 30 minutes.

Strain soup in a colander set over a bowl. Clean pan and return liquid to pan. To clear soup, bring to a boil. Whisk egg white in a small bowl, then stir into soup. Simmer gently 15 minutes.

Strain soup through a muslin-lined sieve set over a bowl. Stir in lemon juice. Cool and refrigerate until chilled. Season soup with salt and pepper. Garnish with lemon slices. Makes 4 to 6 servings.

VICHYSSOISE

2 tablespoons butter
3 medium-size leeks, trimmed, sliced, washed
1 shallot, finely chopped
8 ozs. potatoes, sliced
3 cups light chicken stock
Pinch ground mace or grated nutmeg
Salt and pepper to taste
2/3 cup half and half
Snipped chives to garnish

Melt butter in a large saucepan. Cook leeks and shallot in butter, covered, over low heat 10 minutes without browning. Add potatoes, stock and mace. Bring to a boil, cover and simmer 20 minutes.

In a food processor fitted with a metal blade or a blender, process mixture to a puree. Strain puree through a sieve set over a bowl. Season with salt and pepper.

Cool and stir in 2/3 of half and half. Refrigerate until ready to serve. Swirl in remaining half and half. Garnish soup with snipped chives. Makes 6 servings.

— CHILLED GREEN ONION SOUP —

2 bunches green onions
1 tablespoon olive oil
3-3/4 cups vegetable stock
Salt and pepper to taste
1 hard-cooked egg

Trim green stems from green onions and set aside. Chop white parts. In a large saucepan, saute white parts in oil until soft.

Pour in stock and bring to a boil. Simmer 15 minutes.

Chop green onion stems and stir into soup. Cook 2 minutes, then cool soup. Chill and season with salt and pepper. Chop hard-cooked egg and stir into soup. Makes 4 servings.

SOUP NORMANDE

2 tablespoons butter
1 Spanish onion, chopped
1 teaspoon mild curry powder
1 lb. Red Delicious apples
3 cups chicken stock
Salt and pepper to taste
2 egg yolks
2/3 cup whipping cream
Juice 1/2 lemon
Mint leaves to garnish

Melt butter in a large saucepan. Add onion and saute until soft. Stir in curry powder.

Reserve 1 apple. Peel, core and chop remainder. Stir chopped apples into onion and cook 1 minute. Pour in stock. Bring to a boil, then simmer 20 minutes. In a food processor fitted with a metal blade or a blender, process mixture to a puree. Clean pan and return puree to pan.

In a small bowl, beat egg yolks with whipping cream. Stir into soup and simmer gently until soup thickens. Do not allow soup to boil. Cool and refrigerate at least 2 hours. Peel, core and dice remaining apple and toss in lemon juice. To serve, stir chopped apple into soup. Garnish soup with mint. Makes 4 to 6 servings.

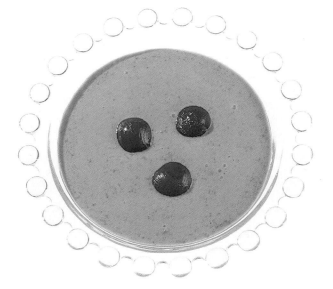

──────── COOL CHERRY SOUP ────────

1-1/2 lbs. ripe black or red cherries
2/3 cup fruity white wine
1 (4-inch) piece cinnamon stick
2/3 cup water
2 tablespoons sugar
Grated peel and juice 1 lemon
1-1/4 cups dairy sour cream
2 tablespoons brandy, if desired

Remove stems and pits from cherries. Crush 1/2 of pits with a mallet.

In a large saucepan, combine crushed pits, whole pits, stems, wine, cinnamon, water, sugar and lemon peel and juice. Bring to a boil, cover and simmer 10 minutes. Strain liquid. Return to pan. Reserve 1/4 of cherries. Stir remaining cherries into strained liquid and simmer 5 minutes.

In a food processor fitted with a metal blade or a blender, process cherry mixture to a puree. Refrigerate until cool, then whisk in sour cream and brandy, if desired. Chill until ready to serve. Garnish soup with reserved cherries. Makes 4 to 6 servings.

—WATERCRESS & ALMOND SOUP—

2 large bunches watercress
2 tablespoons butter
1 small onion
2 cups vegetable stock
1/3 cup blanched almonds, toasted, ground
1 tablespoon plus 1 teaspoon cornstarch
2 cups milk
Salt and pepper to taste
Flaked almonds, lightly toasted, to garnish

Wash watercress. Reserve a few sprigs to garnish. Cut away any coarse stalks and chop remainder.

Melt butter in a large saucepan. Saute onion in butter until soft. Add watercress. Cook 2 minutes, then stir in chicken stock. Cover and simmer 10 minutes.

In a food processor fitted with a metal blade or a blender, process watercress mixture to a puree. Clean pan and return puree to pan. Stir in ground almonds. In a small bowl, blend cornstarch with a little milk. Add to watercress mixture, then stir in remaining milk. Simmer gently over low heat, stirring constantly, 5 minutes or until smooth. Remove from heat and cool. Refrigerate at least 4 hours or overnight. Garnish soup with flaked almonds and reserved watercress sprigs. Makes 4 servings.

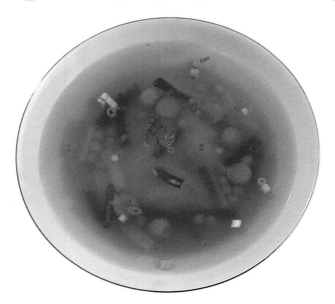

— SUMMER VEGETABLE SOUP —

2/3 cup tomato juice
2-1/2 cups Vegetable Stock, page 74
Grated peel and juice 1/2 lemon
2 large carrots
1/2 red bell pepper, seeded, cut in thin strips
1/2 yellow bell pepper, seeded, cut in thin
    strips
1 oz. freshly shelled green peas
4 green onions, sliced
Fresh chervil to garnish

In a large bowl, combine tomato juice and stock. Whisk in lemon peel and juice. Pour into a soup tureen and refrigerate until chilled.

Cut out tiny balls from carrot with a baller or dice. Blanch carrots, bell peppers and peas in boiling water 2 minutes. Refresh under cold water.

Stir blanched vegetables and green onions into soup. Garnish soup with chervil. Makes 4 servings.

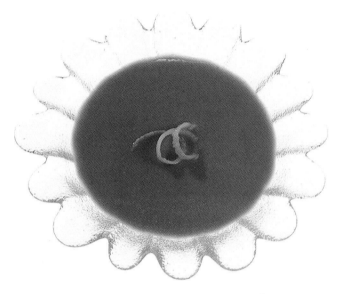

CHILLED PLUM SOUP

1 lb. red plums
2 cups water
2/3 cup fruity white wine
1/3 cup light-brown sugar
1 tablespoon lemon juice
Pinch ground cloves
2/3 cup buttermilk
1/2 teaspoon grated lemon peel
Lemon peel twists to garnish

In a large saucepan, combine plums, water, wine, brown sugar, lemon juice and cloves. Simmer gently about 10 minutes or until plums are tender.

Press mixture through a sieve set over a bowl. Discard skin and pits from plums.

Refrigerate until chilled. Stir in buttermilk and grated lemon peel. Freeze soup 1 hour before serving and serve icy cold. Garnish soup with lemon peel twists. Makes 4 to 6 servings.

PEAR VICHYSSOISE

6 pears
Juice 1/2 lemon
3 cups chicken stock
1 medium-size leek, white part only, chopped
1 medium-size potato, chopped
1/2 teaspoon ground ginger
1/4 cup plus 2 tablespoons cottage cheese,
    sieved
Pinch grated nutmeg
Salt and pepper to taste
Pear slices and watercress leaves to garnish

Peel and core pears. Stir lemon juice into a
large bowl of water. Immerse pears in water.

In a medium-size saucepan, combine skins
and cores of pears and 1/2 of chicken stock.
Simmer a few minutes to extract flavor. Strain
liquid into a large saucepan. Drain pears and
coarsely chop. Stir remaining chicken stock,
chopped pears, leek, potato and ginger into
liquid. Bring to a boil and simmer 20 minutes
or until vegetables are tender.

In a food processor fitted with a metal blade
or a blender, process soup to a puree. Pour
into a large bowl and cool. To serve, whisk
cottage cheese into soup. Garnish soup with
pear slices and watercress leaves. Makes 4 to 6
servings.

SENEGALESE SOUP

2 tablespoons butter
1 small onion, chopped
2 teaspoons mild curry powder
2 tablespoons all-purpose flour
4 cups chicken stock
Juice 1/2 lemon
2/3 cup half and half or plain yogurt
4 ozs. cooked chicken breast, cut in thin strips
Fresh flat-leaf parsley to garnish

Melt butter in a large saucepan. Add onion and simmer gently until soft.

Stir in curry powder and flour and cook 1 minute. Blend in chicken stock and bring to a boil. Simmer 4 minutes. Pour mixture through a sieve set over a bowl. Let stand until cool.

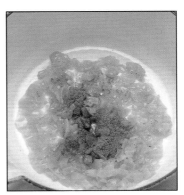

Whisk in lemon juice and half and half. Stir in chicken and refrigerate several hours. Garnish soup with parsley. Makes 4 to 6 servings.

Variation
Substitute 4 ounces of peeled shrimp, coarsely chopped, for chicken.

— CUCUMBER & YOGURT SOUP —

1 large cucumber
1 small onion, chopped
1 tablespoon olive oil
2-1/2 cups hot chicken stock
Grated peel and juice 1/2 lemon
1 tablespoon chopped fresh dill
1/4 cup plus 2 tablespoons plain yogurt
Salt and pepper to taste
Fresh dill sprigs to garnish

Reserve 2 inches of cucumber, then chop remainder. In a large saucepan, saute onion in olive oil until soft. Add chopped cucumber, chicken stock, lemon peel and juice and chopped dill.

Bring to a boil, then cover and simmer 15 to 20 minutes. In a food processor fitted with a metal blade or a blender, process mixture to a puree. Pour into a bowl and cool. Stir in 1/2 of yogurt and refrigerate until chilled.

Season with salt and pepper. Thinly slice reserved piece of cucumber. To serve, float cucumber slices on soup and spoon remaining yogurt on top. Garnish with dill sprigs. Makes 4 to 6 servings

LETTUCE SOUP

2 heads butter lettuce
1 bunch green onions,
1 tablespoon vegetable oil
1 garlic clove, crushed
2 cups chicken stock
2 egg yolks
2/3 cup half and half
Salt and pepper to taste

Trim lettuce, discarding any damaged leaves. Separate and wash leaves. Reserve a few for garnish, then shred remainder.

Heat oil in a large saucepan. Saute green onions and garlic in oil until tender. Add lettuce. Cover and cook until wilted. Pour in chicken stock and bring to a boil, then simmer 15 minutes. Pour through a sieve set over a bowl.

Return mixture to pan. In a small bowl, beat egg yolks and half and half. Stir into soup. Simmer over low heat until soup thickens. Do not allow to boil. Cool and refrigerate until chilled. To serve, roll up reserved lettuce leaves and finely slice. Stir into soup as a garnish. Makes 4 servings.

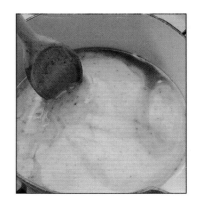

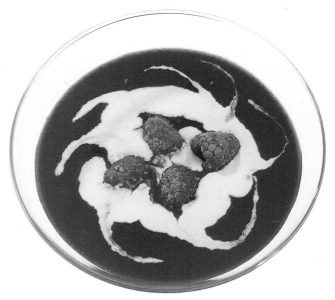

FINNISH BERRY SOUP

**1-1/2 lbs. fresh or frozen mixed berries
(raspberries, red currants, black currants)
1 cup sweet white wine
2 cups water
1 (4-inch) piece cinnamon stick
1/4 cup sugar
1/2 cup whipping cream to garnish**

Select a few good raspberries for garnish and set aside. In a large saucepan, combine remaining berries, wine, water, cinnamon and sugar. Simmer 5 to 10 minutes or until berries are soft.

Remove cinnamon stick and press mixture through a sieve set over a bowl.

Refrigerate at least 1 hour. Lightly whip cream. To serve, swirl whipped cream into soup. Garnish soup with reserved raspberries. Makes 6 servings.

ICED FENNEL SOUP

2 medium-size fennel bulbs, (1 lb. total)
1 tablespoon sunflower oil
1 small onion, chopped
3 cups chicken or vegetable stock
2/3 cup dairy sour cream
Salt and pepper to taste

Remove green feathery leaves from fennel and reserve. Coarsely chop bulbs. Heat oil in a large saucepan over medium heat. Add fennel and onion. Cover and simmer 10 minutes.

Add stock. Bring to a boil. Reduce heat and simmer about 20 minutes or until fennel is tender. Reserve several chopped fennel pieces for garnish.

In a food processor fitted with a metal blade or a blender, process soup to a puree. Cool, then whisk in sour cream. Season with salt and pepper. Chill and check seasoning again before serving. Garnish soup with reserved fennel pieces. Makes 6 servings.

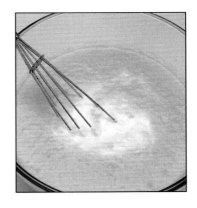

— PROVENÇAL FISH CHOWDER —

1/4 cup virgin olive oil
1 small onion, finely chopped
1 medium-size leek, finely sliced
2 garlic cloves, crushed
12 ozs. ripe tomatoes, peeled, diced
Bouquet garni
1 bay leaf
8 ozs. potatoes, diced
6 cups fish stock
1 tablespoon tomato paste
1-1/2 lbs. white fish, skinned, boned
1/2 teaspoon dried leaf basil
2 ozs. small pitted black olives, cut in half
Salt and pepper to taste

Heat oil in a large saucepan. Saute onion, leek and garlic 5 minutes or until softened. Add tomatoes and cook about 10 minutes or until soft. Add bouquet garni, bay leaf, potatoes, stock and tomato paste. Cover and simmer 15 minutes or until potatoes are just tender.

Cut fish in 1-1/2 inch pieces. Add fish, basil and olives to soup. Season with salt and pepper. Remove bouquet garni and bay leaf before serving. Makes 4 to 6 servings.

——— CREAMY FISH SOUP ———

Stock:
1 lb. fish heads, bones and trimmings
5 cups water
1 small onion, quartered
1 carrot, sliced
1 stalk celery, chopped
Bouquet garni
Salt to taste
6 black peppercorns
1 bay leaf
Lemon slice

Soup:
12 ozs. white fish fillets, skinned
3 tablespoons butter
1/3 cup all-purpose flour
2/3 cup half and half
Salt and pepper to taste
Lemon slices, chopped fresh dill or chervil
    sprigs and paprika to garnish

To prepare stock, combine fish bits, water, vegetables and bouquet garni in a large saucepan. Season with salt. Add peppercorns, bay leaf and lemon slice. Bring to a boil over low heat and skim off any scum that rises to surface. Simmer 20 minutes. Strain stock, without pressing it, through a colander set in a bowl. Clean pan and measure 3-3/4 cups of stock into pan (any remaining can be frozen). Add fish and poach until it flakes.

In a food processor fitted with a metal blade or a blender, process fish and a small amount of stock to a puree. Clean pan and melt butter in pan. Stir in flour and cook 1 minute without browning. Gradually add remainder of stock, then stir until boiling. Simmer 10 minutes. Whisk in fish puree and half and half. Season with salt and pepper. Garnish with lemon slices, chopped dill and paprika. Makes 4 to 6 servings.

— SMOKED HADDOCK CHOWDER —

1 lb. smoked haddock fillets, skinned
2 tablespoons butter
1 medium-size onion, chopped
2 cups fish stock
8 ozs. potatoes, diced
1 carrot, diced
1 bay leaf
1 tablespoon plus 1 teaspoon cornstarch
2 cups milk
1 cup fresh white bread crumbs
Squeeze lemon juice
Pepper to taste
Chopped fresh parsley to garnish

Cut fish in 1-inch pieces.

Melt butter in a large saucepan. Cook onion in butter over low heat until soft. Add stock, potato, carrot and bay leaf. Cover and simmer 15 minutes or until potatoes are just tender.

In a small bowl, blend cornstarch with a small amount of milk. Stir into soup with remaining milk and fish. Simmer gently 8 to 10 minutes or until fish is done. Do not allow to boil or fish will disintegrate. Remove bay leaf. Stir in bread crumbs and lemon juice. Season with pepper. Sprinkle with parsley. Makes 6 servings.

MUSSEL CHOWDER

2 lbs. fresh mussels, well scrubbed, beards
   removed
1-1/4 cups water
1 small onion, finely chopped
1 small green bell pepper, seeded, finely
   chopped
1 garlic clove, crushed
1 tablespoon olive oil
12 ozs. ripe tomatoes, peeled, chopped
1 bay leaf
1 teaspoon dried leaf thyme
Salt and pepper to taste

Place mussels and water in a large saucepan.

Cover and bring to a boil. Cook gently, shak-
ing pan once during cooking, until mussel
shells have opened. Drain mussels, reserving
liquid. Discard any unopened mussels. Reserve 8 small mussels in shells for garnish.
Remove remaining mussels from shells.
Clean pan and heat oil. Gently cook onion,
bell pepper and garlic in oil 5 minutes. Add
tomatoes, bay leaf and thyme. Season with
salt and pepper. Cook 3 minutes. Add
enough water to reserved liquid to measure
2-1/2 cups. Pour into vegetables. Cover and
simmer 15 minutes.

Add shelled mussels to soup and cook 5 min-
utes. Remove bay leaf and check seasoning.
Garnish with reserved mussels in shells.
Makes 4 servings.

CREAM OF SHRIMP SOUP

1 lb. unpeeled shrimp
1/4 cup butter
1 small onion, chopped
1/3 cup all-purpose flour
3 tablespoons dry white wine
2/3 cup half and half

Stock:
8 ozs. fish scraps and bones
1 strip lemon peel
1 stalk celery, chopped
1 small onion, quartered
5 fennel seeds
4 cups water
Salt and pepper to taste

Peel shrimp and reserve. In a large saucepan, combine shrimp shells with all stock ingredients. Slowly bring to a boil and remove any scum which rises to surface. Reduce heat and simmer 25 minutes. Strain through a muslin-lined sieve set over a bowl. Clean pan and return stock to clean pan. Simmer until stock is reduced to 3 cups.

Melt butter in saucepan. Gently cook onion in butter until soft. Stir in flour, then gradually blend in stock. Stir in wine and 3/4 of shrimp. Bring to a boil, then simmer 10 minutes. Cool soup slightly. In a food processor fitted with a metal blade or a blender, process soup to a puree. Clean pan and return puree to pan. Stir in half and half. Season with salt and pepper. Gently reheat 3 to 4 minutes. Garnish soup with reserved shrimp. Makes 4 servings.

CARIBBEAN FISH SOUP

12 ozs. fresh tuna or swordfish steaks
Juice 1 lime
1 green chili pepper, seeded, finely chopped
2 garlic cloves, crushed
2 tablespoons sunflower oil
1 small onion, finely chopped
1 green bell pepper, seeded, diced
1 red bell pepper, seeded, diced
2/3 cup dry white wine
3 cups fish stock
1 teaspoon light-brown sugar
2 tomatoes, peeled, diced
1 small ripe mango, peeled, diced
Salt and pepper to taste

Cut fish in 1-inch pieces and place in a glass dish. Pour over lime juice and stir in chili pepper and garlic. Cover and refrigerate 1 hour. Heat oil in a large saucepan. Cook onion and bell peppers 5 minutes over medium heat. Stir in wine, stock and brown sugar and simmer 15 minutes.

Stir in tomatoes, mango and fish with marinade. Simmer gently 10 minutes. Season with salt and pepper and serve hot. Makes 4 to 6 servings.

SOUPE DE POISSONS

Rouille:
2 slices bread, soaked in milk
3 garlic cloves
1 teaspoon paprika
1/4 teaspoon cayenne pepper
1/4 cup plus 1 tablespoon olive oil
1 tablespoon plus 1 teaspoon tomato paste

Soup:
1/4 cup plus 1 tablespoon olive oil
White part 2 leeks, sliced
2-1/2 lbs. mixture of fish (whiting, cod,
     haddock), cut in chunks
8 ozs. small unpeeled shrimp
2 garlic cloves, chopped
1 lb. ripe tomatoes, chopped
Bouquet garni
1/4 teaspoon saffron threads
6 cups water or fish stock
Salt and pepper to taste
Thin slices oven-dried French bread and
     shredded Gruyère cheese to garnish

To prepare rouille, squeeze milk from bread.
In a mortar, pound soaked bread and garlic to
a paste. Add paprika and cayenne, then add
oil drop by drop until blended. Beat in tomato
paste. To prepare soup, heat oil in a very
large saucepan. Cook leeks in oil until soft.
Stir in shrimp and fish, turning in oil to coat.
Cook over high heat until beginning to
brown. Stir in garlic and tomatoes. Cover and
cook gently 10 minutes. Add bouquet garni,
saffron and water. Bring to a boil and simmer
30 minutes.

Remove bouquet garni. Strain soup. In a
blender, process solids and a small amount of
stock to a puree. Pour mixture through a
sieve set over a bowl. Add 1/4 cup of fish soup
to rouille and mix until smooth. Clean pan
and reheat soup. Season with salt and pepper.
Spread rouille on bread and top with cheese.
Garnish soup with bread. Makes 6 servings.

NEW ENGLAND CLAM CHOWDER

2 (10-oz.) cans clams
3 slices bacon, diced
1 medium-size onion, finely chopped
1 lb. potatoes, diced
1-1/4 cups fish stock
1-1/4 cups milk
2/3 cup half and half
Pinch dried leaf thyme
Salt and pepper to taste

Drain clams, reserving liquid. Chop clams and set aside.

Fry bacon in a large saucepan over high heat until fat runs and bacon in lightly browned. Add onion and saute until soft. Stir in reserved clam liquid, potatoes, stock and milk. Bring to a boil and simmer about 20 minutes or until potatoes are tender.

Stir in clams, half and half, and thyme. Season with salt and pepper. Reheat a few minutes, but do not allow to boil. Makes 6 servings.

SHRIMP BISQUE

8 ozs. unpeeled shrimp
1/4 cup butter
1 small onion, finely chopped
2/3 cup dry white wine
3-3/4 cups water
1 fish stock cube
1 bay leaf
Fresh parsley sprigs
3 strips lemon peel
1 tablespoon tomato paste
Salt and pepper to taste
1/4 cup all-purpose flour
Grated nutmeg
2/3 cup half and half

Peel a few shrimp and reserve for garnish.

Process remaining shrimp in a food processor fitted with a metal blade or a blender until finely chopped. Melt 1/2 of butter in a large saucepan. Gently cook onion in butter until soft. Stir in chopped shrimp and cook 4 to 5 minutes. Pour in wine and boil 2 minutes. Add water, stock cube, bay leaf, parsley, lemon peel and tomato paste. Season with salt and pepper and bring to a boil. Simmer, uncovered, 30 minutes, skimming off any froth that forms on surface. Pour mixture through a sieve set over a bowl. Discard bay leaf and parsley. In a food processor fitted with a metal blade or a blender, process solids in sieve and a small amount of liquid to a puree.

Clean sieve and pour puree through sieve into liquid. Clean pan and melt remaining butter. Stir in flour and cook 1 minute. Gradually blend in liquid. Stir in nutmeg and season with salt and pepper. Bring to a boil, stirring constantly. Simmer 3 minutes. Stir in 1/2 of half and half. Swirl remaining half and half on top of soup. Garnish with reserved shrimp. Makes 4 servings.

BOURRIDE

Aioli:
4 garlic cloves
2 egg yolks
Pinch salt
1-1/4 cups olive oil

Soup:
2 lbs. firm white fish
2 leeks, sliced
2 garlic cloves
2 tomatoes, chopped
Orange peel strip
Bouquet garni
2/3 cup dry white wine
3-3/4 cups water or fish stock
Salt and peppper to taste
4 egg yolks
1/2 thin French bread, thinly sliced, dried in
    oven

To prepare aioli, pound garlic to a pulp in a mortar or crush with a garlic press and mash to a pulp with a wooden spoon. Place garlic in a small bowl and beat in egg yolks and salt. Add oil drop by drop, beating constantly. When 1/3 of oil has been used, add remainder more quickly until a thick mayonnaise is made. To prepare soup, clean fish and cut in large pieces. Place leeks, garlic, tomatoes, orange peel and bouquet garni in a large saucepan. Lay fish on top. Add wine and water and season with salt and pepper. Bring to a boil, then gently cook 10 to 15 minutes. Carefully remove fish and keep warm.

Strain stock through a sieve set over a bowl. In a large bowl, beat egg yolks into 1/2 of aioli. Add hot stock, whisking constantly. Clean pan and return soup to clean pan. Stir over low heat until soup thickens slightly. Do not allow soup to boil. To serve, arrange some bread slices in each soup bowl. Add fish and pour in soup. Spread extra slices of bread with remaining aioli and serve separately. Makes 6 servings.

TUNA & CORN BISQUE

2 tablespoons butter
1 small onion, finely chopped
1 teaspoon mild curry powder
1 teaspoon paprika
1/4 cup all-purpose flour
2 cups chicken stock
2 cups milk
Grated peel 1/2 lemon
1 (12-oz.) can whole kernel corn, drained
1 (7-oz.) can tuna, drained
1 tablespoon chopped fresh parsley and 1/2 cup
  shredded Cheddar cheese (2 ozs.) to garnish

Melt butter in a large saucepan and gently cook onion in butter until soft.

Stir in curry powder, paprika and flour and cook 1 minute. Gradually add stock and bring to a boil, stirring constantly. Stir in milk, lemon peel and corn and simmer 5 minutes.

Stir in tuna, breaking it in flakes, and simmer 5 minutes. Garnish with parsley and grated cheese. Makes 4 servings.

— SCALLOP & ARTICHOKE SOUP —

1-1/4 lbs. Jerusalem artichokes
1 tablespoon lemon juice
1/4 cup butter
1 small onion, chopped
1 medium-size potato, diced
2-1/2 cups chicken stock
6 medium-size scallops
1-1/4 cups milk
Salt and pepper to taste
1/4 cup whipping cream
Chervil sprigs to garnish

Peel and slice artichokes. Stir lemon juice into a bowl of water. Place artichokes in lemon water.

Melt 3/4 of butter in a large saucepan. Drain artichokes. Gently cook artichokes and onion, covered, 10 minutes. Add potato and stock and bring to a boil. Simmer 15 to 20 minutes or until artichokes are soft. In a food processor fitted with a metal blade or a blender, process mixture to a puree. Clean pan and return puree to pan.

Cut white parts of scallops in small pieces, reserving corals. Stir scallops and milk into soup. Simmer a few minutes and season with salt and pepper. Melt remaining butter in a small skillet. Gently saute reserved scallop corals until firm. Slice corals in half. Stir whipping cream into soup and heat gently. Garnish soup with corals and chervil sprigs. Makes 4 servings.

— VIETNAMESE SHRIMP SOUP —

8 ozs. unpeeled cooked shrimp
1 bulb lemon grass, split in half lengthwise
1 (2-inch) piece gingerroot, peeled
3-3/4 cups light chicken stock
1 tablespoon lime juice
1/2 teaspoon crushed dried red chilies
1 tablespoon nam pla (fish sauce) or soy sauce
4 ozs. bok choy leaves, finely shredded

Peel shrimp and set aside. In a large saucepan, combine shells, lemon grass, gingerroot and stock. Bring to a boil. Simmer 5 minutes, then let stand 15 minutes.

Strain stock through a sieve set over a bowl. Clean pan and return stock to pan. Stir in lime juice, red chilies, nam pla and bok choy. Simmer 2 minutes.

Stir shrimp into soup and cook 1 minute. Makes 4 servings.

CRAB & CORN SOUP

3-3/4 cups chicken stock
1 small piece gingerroot, peeled
2 teaspoons light soy sauce
1 tablespoon dry sherry
1 (15-oz.) can creamed corn
Salt and pepper to taste
2 teaspoons cornstarch
2 tablespoons water
4 ozs. crabmeat
2 eggs, beaten
2 green onions, finely sliced, to garnish

In a large saucepan, combine stock and gingerroot. Simmer 15 minutes. Remove gingerroot and stir in soy sauce, sherry and creamed corn. Season with salt and pepper. Simmer 5 minutes.

In a small bowl, blend cornstarch and water. Stir into stock mixture. Stir in crabmeat and heat until mixture thickens.

Bring mixture to a slow simmer and slowly pour in beaten eggs in a thin stream, stirring constantly. Do not allow soup to boil. Garnish soup with sliced green onions. Makes 4 to 6 servings.

STRACCIATELLA

5 cups well-flavored chicken stock
2 eggs
3 tablespoons freshly grated Parmesan cheese
1 tablespoon semolina
2 teaspoons chopped fresh parsley
Pinch grated nutmeg
Salt to taste

Bring stock to a boil in a large saucepan. Meanwhile, beat eggs in a medium-size bowl. Stir in cheese, semolina, parsley and nutmeg. Season with salt.

When stock comes to a bubbling boil, pour in egg mixture, stirring constantly.

Reduce heat and simmer 2 to 3 minutes. Egg will form long threads but may look like small flakes in broth. Serve at once while hot. Makes 4 servings.

CELERY & STILTON SOUP

1 head celery
1 medium-size onion, chopped
3 tablespoons butter
3-3/4 cups light vegetable or chicken stock
2 egg yolks
2/3 cup half and half
1 cup crumbled Blue Stilton cheese (4 oz.)
Salt and pepper to taste

Blue Cheese Croutons:
2 tablespoons butter, softened
1/3 cup shredded blue cheese (1 oz.)
1 thick slice bread

Reserve inner leaves from celery and chop remaining celery. Melt butter in a large saucepan. Gently cook celery and onion in butter, covered, until soft. Add stock and bring to a boil. Simmer 20 minutes or until vegetables are tender. Cool slightly. In a food processor fitted with a metal blade or a blender, process mixture to a puree. Clean pan and return puree to pan. Reheat gently without bringing to a boil.

Meanwhile, to prepare croutons, beat butter and shredded cheese in a small bowl. Toast bread. Spread cheese-butter on 1 side and broil until cheese-butter melts. Cut in small squares. To finish soup, beat egg yolks and half and half in a small bowl. Stir a small ladleful of hot soup into egg mixture and pour back into pan. Stir in crumbled cheese, stirring constantly until soup thickens. Season with salt and pepper. Garnish with reserved celery leaves and croutons and serve hot. Makes 4 to 6 servings.

— POTAGE CRÈME DE FROMAGE —

2 tablespoons butter
1 medium-size onion, finely chopped
1 stalk celery, finely chopped
1/4 cup all-purpose flour
2 cups hot chicken stock
2/3 cup milk
4 ozs. Camembert cheese, rind removed
1/2 cup cottage cheese, sieved
Salt and pepper to taste

Parsley Croutons:
1 thick slice white bread, crusts removed
Butter
2 tablespoons finely chopped fresh parsley

Melt butter in a large saucepan. Gently cook onion and celery in butter 5 minutes. Stir in flour and cook 1 minute. Gradually stir in stock and milk. Gradually bring to a simmer and cook 15 minutes. Meanwhile, toast bread on both sides until golden. Cool and spread with butter. Cut in small squares and toss in chopped parsley.

Cut cheese in small pieces. Add cheese and cottage cheese to soup. Stir 2 to 3 minutes or until cheese is melted. Season with salt and pepper. Garnish soup with parsley croutons. Makes 4 servings.

PAVIA SOUP

5 cups chicken consommé, page 96
1/3 cup butter
2 slices firm bread
1/4 cup freshly grated Parmesan cheese
    (3/4 oz.)
12 quail eggs
Flat-leaf parsley to garnish
Additional freshly grated Parmesan cheese, if
    desired

Simmer consommé in a large saucepan. Melt butter in a large skillet. Fry bread on both sides until golden, then cut each slice in 6 pieces. Sprinkle fried bread with grated cheese.

Carefully break quail eggs into consommé, cooking 3 or 4 at a time. When set, remove eggs with a slotted spoon onto pieces of fried bread.

Place 3 pieces of fried bread with quail eggs in each soup bowl, then strain hot consommé into each. Garnish with parsley and serve with grated cheese, if desired. Makes 4 servings.

OMELETTE SOUP

5 cups chicken stock
3 eggs
1 tablespoons all-purpose flour
1/4 cup plus 2 tablespoons milk
Salt to taste
2 tablespoons freshly grated Parmesan cheese

In a large saucepan, bring stock to a boil. In a small bowl, beat eggs, flour, milk and salt.

Lightly grease bottom of a 7-inch skillet. Pour 1/3 of egg mixture into skillet. Cook until set and golden. Turn out onto a plate and roll up, jelly-roll style. Prepare 2 more omelettes.

Cut omelettes in thin strips. Add to stock. Reheat gently and sprinkle with grated cheese. Makes 4 servings.

AVGOLÉMONO

5 cups chicken stock
Salt and pepper to taste
1/3 cup long-grain white rice
2 eggs
Finely grated peel 1/2 lemon
Juice 1 lemon
3 tablespoons chopped fresh parsley
Thin lemon slices and fresh flat-leaf parsley
    leaves to garnish

Bring stock to a boil in a large saucepan. Season with salt and pepper. Stir in rice, cover and simmer 15 minutes or until rice is tender.

In a small bowl, beat eggs and lemon peel and juice. Whisk a ladleful of hot stock into egg mixture, then pour mixture back into stock, stirring constantly.

Reheat over low heat until soup thickens and looks creamy. Do not allow to boil. Stir in chopped parsley. Garnish with lemon slices and parsley leaves and serve at once. Or serve soup cold, if desired. Makes 4 to 6 servings.

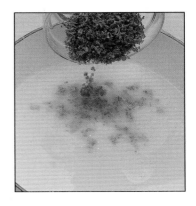

—— PLOUGHMAN'S SOUP ——

3 tablespoons butter
2 medium-size onions, chopped
1/4 cup whole-wheat flour
2 cups chicken stock
1 cup light ale
Dash Worcestershire sauce
1-1/2 cups crumbled Cheshire cheese (6 oz.)
Salt and pepper to taste
Mild raw onion rings to garnish

Melt butter in a large saucepan. Gently cook onion until soft. Stir in whole-wheat flour and cook 1 minute.

Remove from heat and gradually blend in stock and ale. Return to heat and bring to a boil. Simmer 5 minutes or until thickened. Stir in Worcestershire sauce.

Reserve 1/4 cup cheese. Stir in remaining cheese, a little at a time, over a low heat until cheese is melted. Season with salt and pepper. Garnish with reserved cheese and onion rings. Makes 4 servings.

PASSATELLI

5 cups well-flavored chicken stock
4 eggs
1 cup freshly grated Parmesan cheese (3 oz.)
1 cup fine dry white bread crumbs
1/4 teaspoon grated nutmeg
2 tablespoons butter, softened
Salt and pepper to taste

Bring stock to a boil in a large saucepan.

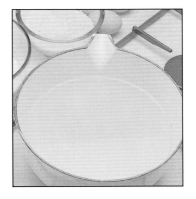

Beat eggs in a medium-size bowl. Stir in cheese, bread crumbs, nutmeg and butter. Season with salt and pepper. Mix to make a stiff paste.

Press paste through a colander into boiling stock. Cook 1 to 2 minutes or until threads of noodles rise to surface. Remove from heat and let stand 5 minutes before serving. Makes 4 servings.

—— FENNEL & WALNUT SOUP ——

Sage Derby Puffs:
3 tablespoons water
2 tablespoons butter
1/4 cup all-purpose flour
1/2 egg, beaten
3/4 cup shredded Sage Derby cheese (3 oz.)
Salt and pepper to taste
1/2 (4-oz.) pkg. cream cheese
2 tablespoons half and half

Soup:
1 tablespoon vegetable oil
1 medium-size onion, chopped
1 large bulb fennel, trimmed, chopped
3-3/4 cups vegetable stock
2 oz. walnuts, chopped
Salt and pepper to taste

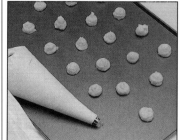

To prepare puffs, preheat oven to 400F (200C). Grease a baking sheet. In a medium-size saucepan, bring water and butter to a boil. Remove from heat and beat in flour until smooth. Cool slightly, then beat in egg. Stir in 1/2 of cheese. Season with salt and pepper. In a pastry bag fitted with a small plain nozzle, pipe pea-size rounds onto greased baking sheet. Bake in preheated oven 7 to 10 minutes or until crisp. Cool slightly, then cut a slit in each round with point of a sharp knife. To prepare soup, heat oil in a large saucepan. Gently cook onion and fennel in oil until soft. Add stock and bring to a boil, then simmer 20 minutes.

Meanwhile, beat remaining cheese, cream cheese and half and half in a small bowl. Fill slits in puffs. In a food processor fitted with a metal blade or a blender, grind walnuts. Transfer ground nuts to a small dish. In food processor or blender, process soup to a smooth puree. Clean pan and return puree to pan. Stir in ground nuts and season with salt and pepper. Gently reheat. Garnish with puffs. Makes 4 to 6 servings.

─── CHICKEN EGG DROP SOUP ───

1 tablespoon plus 2 teaspoons cornstarch
3 tablespoons rice wine
1 tablespoon soy sauce
5 cups chicken stock
1/2 teaspoon sugar
8 ozs. cooked chicken breast, diced
6 green onions, shredded
2 eggs
1 tablespoon plus 1 teaspoon all-purpose flour
Green onion curls to garnish

In a large saucepan, combine cornstarch, wine and soy sauce. Pour in stock and slowly bring to a boil. Simmer 2 minutes.

Add chicken and shredded green onions and simmer 2 to 3 minutes.

In a small bowl, beat eggs and flour. While stock is simmering, pour egg mixture through a sieve into stock. Simmer 1 minute, stirring stock as egg drops into pan. Garnish with green onion curls. Makes 4 to 6 servings.

TOMATO & RICE SOUP

1 small onion, chopped
2 garlic cloves, crushed
1 (1-lb./12-oz.) can tomatoes
2 tablespoons tomato paste
1 tablespoon chopped fresh basil or 1/2
    teaspoon dried leaf basil
2-1/2 cups water
1 teaspoon sugar
1/3 cup long-grain white rice
3 tablespoons dry sherry
Salt and pepper to taste
Fresh basil leaves to garnish

In a large saucepan, combine onion, garlic, tomatoes with juice, tomato paste, chopped basil, water and sugar. Bring to a boil, cover and simmer 30 minutes. In a food processor fitted with a metal blade or a blender, process tomato mixture to a puree. Clean pan. Pour puree through a sieve set over clean pan.

Bring back to a boil and add rice. Reduce heat and simmer 15 minutes or until rice is tender. Stir in sherry and season with salt and pepper. Garnish with basil leaves. Makes 4 to 6 servings.

— COUNTRY MUSHROOM SOUP —

1 medium-size onion, thinly sliced
1/3 cup brown rice
6 cups chicken stock
3 tablespoons butter
1 lb. fresh mushrooms, wiped clean, trimmed,
    sliced
1/4 cup plus 1 tablespoon dry sherry
Salt and pepper to taste
Fresh parsley sprigs to garnish

In a large saucepan, combine onion, brown rice and stock. Bring to a boil, then simmer 25 minutes.

Meanwhile, melt butter in a large saucepan. Gently cook mushrooms about 10 minutes or until golden brown and most of moisture has evaporated.

Add mushrooms to stock. Stir in sherry and season with salt and pepper. Simmer 10 minutes. Garnish with parsley sprigs and serve hot. Makes 6 servings.

Variation: Use 2 or more varieties of mushrooms (button and open or chestnut mushrooms) which have a very good flavor. Wild mushrooms can be used if available.

—— ROSEMARY & LENTIL SOUP ——

6 ozs. green lentils, soaked overnight
7-1/2 cups vegetable stock
1 medium-size potato, diced
2 stalks celery, diced
1 garlic clove, crushed
Large fresh rosemary sprig
Salt and pepper to taste
Additional fresh rosemary sprigs to garnish

Sausage Dumplings:
3 ozs. pork sausage
1/4 cup all-purpose flour
1/2 teaspoon mixed herbs
1/2 small egg, beaten

Drain lentils and place in a large saucepan. Add stock and slowly bring to a boil. Skim off any scum which rises to surface and simmer 15 minutes. Add potato, celery, garlic and large rosemary sprig. Season with salt and pepper and simmer 30 minutes. Remove rosemary sprig. In a food processor fitted with a metal blade or a blender, process mixture to a puree.

Clean pan and return puree to pan. Slowly reheat while preparing dumplings. Combine all dumpling ingredients in a medium-size bowl. When soup simmers, drop spoonfuls of dumplings into soup, keeping them apart. Cover and cook soup 15 minutes. Garnish with rosemary sprigs. Makes 6 servings.

— ITALIAN BEAN & PASTA SOUP —

2 tablespoons olive oil
1 medium-size onion, finely chopped
1 garlic clove, crushed
2 celery stalks finely sliced
1 carrot, finely diced
1 tablespoon tomato paste
5 cups beef stock
1 (15-oz.) can red kidney beans, drained
3 ozs. small pasta shapes
4 ozs. frozen green peas
Salt and pepper to taste

Heat oil in a large saucepan. Add onion, garlic, celery and carrot. Stir and cook gently 5 minutes.

Add tomato paste, stock and beans. Bring to a boil and simmer 10 minutes.

Add pasta and peas and cook another 7 minutes or until pasta is just cooked. Season with salt and pepper. Makes 4 to 6 servings.

SPICY LENTIL SOUP

2 tablespoons olive oil
1/2 teaspoon cumin seeds
1 medium-size onion, chopped
1 garlic clove, crushed
2 carrots, chopped
2 stalks celery, chopped
1/2 teaspoon chili powder
1/2 teaspoon turmeric
1 teaspoon ground coriander
6 oz. red lentils, washed
5 cups vegetable stock
1 bay leaf
Salt and pepper to taste
Fried onion rings and fresh tarragon sprigs to
   garnish

Heat oil in a large saucepan over medium heat. Add cumin seeds. When seeds begin to pop, add onion and cook until golden. Add garlic, carrots and celery and cook gently 10 minutes. Stir in all spices and cook 1 minute, then add lentils.

Pour in stock. Add bay leaf and bring to a boil. Reduce heat and simmer 1 hour. Remove bay leaf. In a food processor fitted with a metal blade or a blender, process soup to a puree. Clean pan and return puree to pan. Season with salt and pepper. Gently reheat. Garnish with fried onion rings and tarragon sprigs. Makes 6 servings.

—— WHITE BEAN SOUP ——

8 ozs. navy or cannellini beans,
   soaked overnight
3-3/4 cups chicken stock
3-3/4 cups water
Salt and pepper to taste
2 tablespoons olive oil
1 garlic clove, crushed
2 tablespoons chopped fresh parsley
1 tablespoon diced red bell pepper and 1
   tablespoon diced green bell pepper to
   garnish
Additional olive oil, if desired

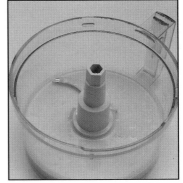

Drain beans. In a large saucepan, combine drained beans, stock and water.

Bring to a boil. Half-cover pan and simmer 2 to 2-1/2 hours or until beans are tender. In a food processor fitted with a metal blade or a blender, process 1/2 of beans to a puree, or press through a sieve set over a bowl. Stir puree back into remaining beans.

Heat oil in a small saucepan. Gently cook garlic until soft. Do not allow to brown. Stir garlic and parsley into soup and reheat slowly. Meanwhile, blanch diced bell peppers in boiling water 2 minutes and drain. Garnish soup with bell peppers. If desired, pour additional oil over soup. Makes 4 to 6 servings.

—— BLACK BEAN SOUP ——

8 ozs. black beans
1 medium-size onion, finely chopped
2 tablespoons vegetable oil
1 bay leaf
5 cups water
5 cups vegetable or chicken stock
1 green or yellow bell pepper, seeded, diced
2 garlic cloves, crushed
1/3 cup brown rice
Salt and pepper to taste
4 ozs. ham, diced

Wash and pick over beans. Place beans in a large saucepan and cover with water.

Bring to a boil and boil 2 minutes. Cover and let stand 2 hours. Drain beans. Clean pan and heat oil in clean pan. Cook onion in oil until brown. Add beans, bay leaf and water. Bring to a boil, cover and simmer 1-1/2 hours.

Drain beans, onion and bay leaf. Clean pan and return beans, onion and bay leaf to clean pan. Stir in stock, bell pepper, garlic and rice. Season with salt and pepper. Simmer 1 hour or until beans are tender. Stir in diced ham and season again, if desired. Remove bay leaf. Makes 4 to 6 servings.

DUTCH PEA SOUP

8 ozs. yellow split peas, soaked overnight
6 cups water
Bouquet garni
1 bay leaf
8 slices bacon, diced
1 onion, chopped
2 leeks, chopped
1 large carrot, chopped
2 stalks celery, chopped
Salt and pepper to taste
1 (4-oz.) piece spicy or garlic sausage, diced
2 tablespoons chopped fresh parsley

Drain peas. In a large saucepan, combine peas, water, bouquet garni and bay leaf.

Bring to a boil, cover pan and simmer 2 hours. Stir in diced bacon and vegetables and simmer 1 hour.

Remove bouquet garni and bay leaf. In a food processor fitted with a metal blade or a blender, process soup to a puree. Clean pan and return puree to clean pan. Season with salt and pepper. Stir in sausage and reheat soup. Stir in chopped parsley. Makes 6 servings.

MEXICAN BEAN SOUP

2 tablespoons olive oil
1 medium-size onion, chopped
1 garlic clove, crushed
1 green bell pepper, seeded, diced
12 oz. ripe tomatoes, peeled, chopped
1/2 teaspoon chili powder
3-3/4 cups vegetable stock
2 tablespoons tomato paste
1 (15-oz.) can red kidney beans, drained
Salt and pepper to taste
1 avocado
1 cup whole kernel corn
Few drops hot-pepper sauce
1 tablespoon chopped fresh cilantro
Fresh cilantro sprigs to garnish

Heat oil in a large saucepan. Cook onion until soft. Stir in garlic, bell pepper, tomatoes and chili powder. Cook 3 to 4 minutes. Pour in stock. Add tomato paste and 3/4 of beans. Simmer 30 minutes. Cool slightly. In a food processor fitted with a metal blade or a blender, process mixture to a puree.

Clean pan and return puree to clean pan. Season with salt and pepper. Cut avocado in half. Remove seed, peel and dice. Stir remaining beans, avocado, corn and hot-pepper sauce into puree. Gently reheat soup. Stir in chopped cilantro. Garnish with cilantro sprigs. Makes 4 to 5 servings.

——— HARVEST BARLEY SOUP ———

1/3 cup pearl barley
5 cups vegetable stock
1 large carrot, diced
1 small turnip, diced
1 stalk celery, chopped
1 small onion, finely chopped
2 young leeks, sliced
1/2 teaspoon mixed dried herbs
1 tablespoon plus 2 teaspoons tomato paste
Salt and pepper to taste
1 bay leaf
1 (7-1/2-oz.) can butter beans, drained

Cheesey Croutons:
1 thick slice bread
1/2 cup shredded Cheddar cheese (2 oz.)

In a large saucepan, combine barley and
stock. Bring to a boil and simmer 45 minutes
or until barley is tender. Stir in prepared
vegetables, herbs and tomato paste. Season
with salt and pepper. Add bay leaf. Simmer
20 minutes. To prepare croutons, toast bread
on both sides. Remove crusts and sprinkle
bread with cheese. Broil until cheese is melted
and golden.

Remove bay leaf and stir in beans. Gently
cook 5 minutes to heat through. Cut croutons
in squares and garnish soup. Makes 4 to 6
servings.

POTAGE BONNE FEMME

1/4 cup butter
1 lb. potatoes, diced
2 carrots, chopped
2 large leeks, chopped
7-1/2 cups vegetable stock
Salt and pepper to taste
1/2 cup whipping cream
1 tablespoon finely chopped fresh parsley or
   chervil
1/2 carrot, cut in fine strips, 1/2 small leek, cut
   in fine strips and 1 slice bread, toasted, to
   garnish

Melt butter in a large saucepan. Add prepared vegetables.

Cover and cook gently 15 minutes. Add stock, bring to a boil and simmer 20 minutes. In a food processor fitted with a metal blade or a blender, process mixture to a puree. Pass through a seive set over a bowl. Clean pan and return puree to clean pan. Season with salt and pepper. Stir in whipping cream and parsley and reheat very slowly.

To prepare garnish, blanch carrot and leek strips in boiling salted water 1 minute, then drain. Cut out 4 small rounds from toast. Top toast rounds with blanched vegetables. Garnish soup with blanched vegetables and toast rounds. Makes 4 servings.

— MINORCAN VEGETABLE SOUP —

2 red bell peppers
2 tablespoons olive oil
1 large Spanish onion, chopped
2 garlic cloves, finely chopped
8 ozs. tomatoes, peeled, seeded, chopped
5 cups water
1 small cabbage
1/2 teaspoon dried leaf thyme
1 bay leaf
1 teaspoon paprika
Salt and pepper to taste
8 to 12 slices bread, toasted
2 garlic cloves cut in half

Broil bell peppers until skins are blisted and charred, turning over once.

Place in a plastic bag and let stand 15 minutes. Peel bell peppers, remove tops and seeds and chop. Heat oil in a large saucepan. Add onion and cook until soft. Add bell peppers, garlic and tomatoes. Cover pan and cook gently 15 minutes. Pour in water and bring to a boil.

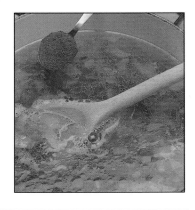

Discard outer leaves of cabbage. Shread remaining cabbage. Add shredded cabbage, thyme, bay leaf and paprika to soup. Simmer 15 minutes. Season with salt and pepper. To serve, rub toast with a cut side of garlic. Place toast in soup bowls, then ladle hot soup over toast. Serve at once. Makes 4 to 6 servings.

— ZUCCHINI & TOMATO SOUP —

2 tablespoons butter
1 medium-size onion, finely chopped
12 ozs. zucchini, coarsely grated
1 garlic clove, crushed
2-1/2 cups vegetable stock
1 (14-oz.) can chopped tomatoes
2 tablespoons chopped fresh mixed herbs, if
　　desired
Salt and pepper to taste
1/4 cup whipping cream and fresh basil leaves
　　to garnish

Melt butter in a large saucepan. Cook onion in butter over medium heat until soft. Stir in zucchini and garlic and cook 4 to 5 minutes.

Stir in stock and tomatoes with juice. Bring to a boil and simmer 15 minutes.

Stir in herbs, if desired, and season with salt and pepper. Garnish with dollops of whipping cream and basil leaves. Makes 4 servings.

CURRIED PARSNIP SOUP

3 tablespoons butter
1 medium-size onion, chopped
1 teaspoon chopped gingerroot
1 teaspoon curry powder
1/2 teaspoon ground cumin
1 lb. parsnips, chopped
1 medium-size potato, chopped
3-3/4 cups beef stock
2/3 cup plain yogurt
Salt and pepper to taste
Lemon peel strips to garnish

Curried Croutons:
1/2 teaspoon curry powder
Squeeze lemon juice
2 tablespoons butter
2 thick slices bread

Melt butter in a large saucepan. Gently cook onion in butter until onion is soft. Stir in gingerroot, curry powder and cumin and cook 1 minute. Add parsnips and potato and stir over medium heat to coat vegetables with spicy butter. Pour in stock and bring to a boil. Simmer 30 minutes or until vegetables are very tender. In a food processor fitted with a metal blade or a blender, process mixture to a puree. Clean pan and return puree to clean pan. Ladle a small amount of puree into a bowl. Whisk in yogurt, then pour back into puree.

Season soup with salt and pepper and gently reheat. To prepare croutons, preheat oven to 400F (205C). In a small bowl, beat curry powder, lemon juice and butter. Spread on bread. Remove crusts and cut in cubes. Place cubes on a baking sheet and bake in preheated oven until crisp and golden. Garnish soup with croutons and lemon peel strips. Makes 4 to 6 servings.

PISTOU

1 tablespoon olive oil
1 medium-size onion, chopped
5 cups water
1 small potato, diced
2 carrots, sliced
2 stalks celery, finely sliced
Bouquet garni
2 small zucchini, sliced
6 ozs. green beans, cut in short lengths
1 oz. broken spaghetti or pasta shells
Salt and pepper to taste

Pistou:
3 garlic cloves
1/4 cup chopped fresh basil leaves
Salt to taste
1/2 cup freshly grated Parmesan cheese
   (1-1/2 ozs.)
2 medium-size tomatoes, peeled, seeded,
   chopped
1/4 cup olive oil

Heat 1 tablespoon oil in a large saucepan. Cook onion in oil until onion is just beginning to color. Pour in water and bring to a boil. Add potato, carrots, celery and bouquet garni. Simmer 10 minutes. Add zucchini, green beans and pasta and simmer uncovered 10 to 15 minutes or until tender.

Meanwhile, to prepare pistou, pound garlic and basil in a mortar with a pestle. Season with salt. Gradually add cheese until mixture becomes a stiff paste, then add about 1/3 of tomatoes. Continue adding cheese and tomatoes alternately, then slowly work in remaining oil to make a thick sauce. Remove bouquet garni from soup. Season with salt and pepper. Serve soup with pistou. Makes 4 to 6 servings.

—CREAM OF CAULIFLOWER SOUP—

1 large cauliflower
1/4 cup butter
1 medium-size onion, chopped
1/4 cup all-purpose flour
2 cups chicken stock
2 cups milk
Salt and pepper to taste
Pinch grated nutmeg
1/4 cup crème fraiche

Cheese Snippets:
2 tablespoons grated Parmesan cheese
3 tablespoons butter
2 medium-size slices bread

Break cauliflower in flowerets.

Blanch cauliflower in boiling salted water 3
minutes, then drain. Melt butter in a large
saucepan. Cook onion in butter until soft. Stir
in flour, then gradually stir in stock. Bring to
a boil and simmer 20 minutes. Strain into
another large saucepan. Stir in milk and add
cauliflower. Season with salt and pepper. Add
nutmeg and simmer 10 minutes. Using a slotted spoon, reserve 1/3 of cauliflower.

In a food processor fitted with a metal blade
or a blender, process mixture to a puree.
Clean pan and return puree to clean pan. Stir
in crème fraiche and reserved cauliflower.
Reheat very slowly. Meanwhile to prepare
snippets, preheat oven to 400F (205C). Beat
cheese and butter in a small bowl. Spread
butter-cheese over bread. Remove crusts,
then cut in small squares or diamonds. Place
on a baking sheet and bake in preheated oven
until golden and crisp. Garnish soup with
snippets. Makes 6 servings.

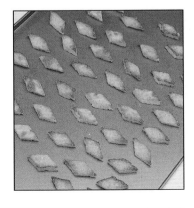

—— CREAM OF CARROT SOUP ——

2 tablespoons butter
1 small onion, finely chopped
1 medium-size potato, diced
1 lb. carrots, chopped
3 cups vegetable stock
Pinch sugar
2/3 cup half and half
Salt and pepper to taste

Herb Croutons:
2 tablespoons butter
1 teaspoon dried leaf herbs
2 slices bread

Melt butter in a large saucepan. Add onion, potato and carrots.

Cover and cook over low heat 10 minutes. Add stock and sugar. Bring to a boil, then simmer 30 minutes. In a food processor fitted with a metal blade or a blender, process mixture to a puree. Clean pan and return puree to clean pan. Stir in half and half and season with salt and pepper.

To prepare croutons, preheat oven to 400F (205C). Beat butter and herbs in a small bowl. Spread herbed butter over bread. Cut in fancy shapes or squares and place on a baking sheet. Bake in preheated oven until crisp and golden. Garnish soup with croutons. Makes 4 servings.

PESTO SOUP

1/4 cup plus 3 tablespoons olive oil
1 small onion, finely chopped
12 ounces zucchini, diced
1/2 cup rissotto rice
5 cups hot chicken stock
Salt and pepper to taste
1 oz. fresh basil leaves
1/4 cup pine nuts
2 garlic cloves
1/4 teaspoon salt
1/2 cup freshly grated Parmesan cheese

Parmesan Croutons:
2 tablespoons butter
2 slices bread

Heat 2 tablespoons of oil in a large saucepan. Gently cook onion and zucchini 3 to 4 minutes or until softened. Stir in rice and coat grains with oil. Pour in hot stock and bring to a boil. Simmer 10 minutes or until rice is tender. Season with salt and pepper. Meanwhile, to prepare pesto sauce, process remaining olive oil, basil leaves, pine nuts, garlic and 1/4 teaspoon salt to a puree in a blender. Transfer mixture to a small bowl and beat in 1/2 of cheese.

To prepare croutons, beat remaining cheese and butter in a small bowl. Toast bread on both sides. Spread toast with cheese-butter and broil until melted and golden. Cut out fancy shapes or remove crusts and dice. Stir 1 heaping tablespoon of pesto sauce into soup. Refrigerate remaining pesto sauce for another use. Garnish soup with croutons. Makes 4 to 5 servings.

MINESTRONE

2 tablespoons olive oil
1 medium-size onion, chopped
1 garlic clove, crushed
1 small leek, sliced
2 carrots, diced
2 stalks celery, sliced
7-1/2 cups chicken or beef stock
1 tablespoon tomato paste
1 (14-oz.) can navy beans, drained
3 tomatoes, peeled, seeded, chopped
2 ozs. green beans, cut in short lengths
2 cups shredded cabbage
1 oz. soup pasta
Salt and pepper to taste
2 tablespoons chopped fresh parsley
Freshly grated Parmesan cheese to garnish

Heat oil in a large saucepan. Cook onion, garlic and leek over low heat 5 minutes. Stir in carrots, celery, stock, tomato paste and drained beans and bring to a simmer. Cover and cook 30 minutes. Stir in tomatoes and green beans and simmer 10 minutes.

Stir in cabbage and pasta. Season with salt and pepper. Cook 10 minutes or until pasta is tender. Stir in parsley. Garnish with cheese. Makes 6 servings.

FRENCH TURNIP SOUP

2 tablespoons butter
1 lb. small white turnips
1 small onion, chopped
5 cups vegetable stock
4 slices white bread, crusts removed
4 ozs. shelled fresh green peas
Salt and pepper to taste
Pinch grated nutmeg

Cheese Puffs:
4 ozs. puff pastry
3 tablespoons cream cheese with herbs and
    garlic
1 egg, beaten

Heat butter in a large saucepan. Add turnips and onion.

Cook gently 10 minutes or until they begin to soften. Add stock and bread and simmer gently 25 minutes. In a food processor fitted with a metal blade or a blender, process mixture to a puree. Clean pan and return puree to clean pan. Blanch peas in boiling salted water 2 minutes, then add peas to soup. Season with salt and pepper. Add nutmeg.

To prepare puffs, preheat oven to 400F (205C). Grease a baking sheet. Roll out pastry thinly and cut in 2-inch rounds. Place 1/2 teaspoon of cheese in center of each round. Dampen edge of pastry, then fold over and place on greased baking sheet. Bake in preheated oven until crisp and golden. Garnish soups with puffs. Makes 4 servings.

— CARROT & CILANTRO SOUP —

1 lb. carrots
2 tablespoons olive oil
1 small onion, finely chopped
1 garlic clove, crushed
1 teaspoon coriander seeds, crushed
1 teaspoon ground coriander
3-3/4 cups vegetable stock
Salt and pepper to taste
1/3 cup dark raisins, chopped
1 tablespoons chopped fresh cilantro

Sesame Croutons:
1 thick slice bread, crusts removed
1 tablespoon butter
1 tablespoon sesame seeds

Dice 2 carrots and set aside. Chop remaining carrots. Heat oil in a large saucepan. Gently cook chopped carrots, onion and garlic in oil 10 minutes. Stir in crushed coriander seeds and ground coriander and cook 1 minute. Pour in 3 cups of stock. Cover, bring to a simmer and cook 15 minutes or until carrots are tender. Meanwhile, in a small saucepan, simmer diced carrots in remaining stock until carrots are tender.

In a food processor fitted with a metal blade or a blender, process mixture to a puree. Clean pan and return puree to clean pan. Stir cooked diced carrots with stock and raisins into puree. Season with salt and pepper. Reheat gently. To prepare croutons, toast bread on each side until golden. Cool, spread with butter and sprinkle with sesame seeds. Toast until golden. Cut toast in small cubes. Stir chopped cilantro into soup. Garnish soup with sesame seed croutons. Makes 4 servings.

GARLIC SOUP

3 tablespoons butter
6 garlic cloves
1/4 cup all-purpose flour
2-1/2 cups chicken stock
2/3 cup dry white wine
1 teaspoon dried leaf thyme
Salt and pepper to taste
1 egg yolk
2/3 cup half and half
3/4 cup ground almonds
Seedless green grapes, cut in half, to garnish

Melt butter in a large saucepan. Slightly crush garlic. Cook garlic in butter over low heat 3 to 4 minutes or until golden.

Stir in flour, then gradually blend in stock. Stir in wine and thyme. Season with salt and pepper and simmer 10 minutes. In a large bowl, beat egg yolk and half and half . Strain stock mixture into bowl, whisking constantly.

Clean pan and return mixture to clean pan. Stir in almonds and reheat without boiling. Garnish soup with grapes. Makes 4 servings.

— HUNGARIAN CABBAGE SOUP —

2 tablespoons vegetable oil
3 cups shredded red cabbage
1 medium-size onion, finely sliced
1 garlic clove, crushed
1/2 teaspoon caraway seeds
1 (14-oz.) can tomatoes, sieved
1 tablespoon red wine vinegar
3-3/4 cups chicken or veal stock
Salt and pepper to taste
1/4 cup plus 2 tablespoons sour cream
1 tablespoon chopped fresh dill
Fresh dill sprigs to garnish

In a large saucepan, combine oil, cabbage and onion.

Cover and cook over medium heat about 20 minutes or until cabbage is soft. Stir in garlic, caraway seeds, tomatoes, vinegar and stock. Season with salt and gently simmer 30 minutes.

In a small bowl, combine dill and sour cream. Season soup with pepper and top portions of soup with dilled sour cream. Garnish with dill sprigs. Makes 4 to 6 servings.

—— WINTER VEGETABLE SOUP ——

2 tablespoons butter
1 medium-size onion, sliced
8 ozs. carrots, diced
8 ozs. rutabagas, diced
1 medium-size potato, diced
2 large parsnips, diced
2 cups vegetable stock
1 bay leaf
1 tablespoon cornstarch
2 cups milk
Salt and pepper to taste
1 cup frozen green peas
2 small bread rolls
1/2 cup shredded Cheddar cheese (2 oz.)

Melt butter in a large saucepan. Add onion, carrots, rutabagas, potato and parsnips. Cover and cook over low heat 10 minutes. Add stock and bay leaf and simmer 30 minutes. In a small bowl, blend cornstarch with a small amount of milk, then add to soup. Pour remaining milk into soup and heat, stirring until soup thickens. Remove bay leaf and season with salt and pepper.

Stir green peas into soup and simmer over low heat. Cut bread rolls in half. Sprinkle with cheese. Broil until cheese is melted. Serve bread rolls with soup. Makes 4 servings.

CLEAR VEGETABLE SOUP

2 carrots, thinly sliced
2 stalks celery, sliced
2 ozs. button mushrooms, sliced
1-1/4 cups broccoli flowerets
1/2 cup frozen green peas
1 zucchini, cut in strips
Salt and pepper to taste
Fresh flat-leaf parsley sprigs to garnish

Vegetable Stock:
1 small onion, thinly sliced
1 leek, chopped
2 stalks celery, chopped
3 carrots, chopped
2 tomatoes, chopped
5 cups water
Bouquet garni
2 bay leaves
Salt to taste
1/2 teaspoon black peppercorns

To prepare stock, combine all stock ingredients in a large saucepan. Bring to a boil and simmer 40 minutes. For a stronger flavor, boil rapidly 5 minutes or until stock is reduced to 3-3/4 cups. Strain stock into a large bowl. Clean pan and return strained stock to clean pan. Add carrots, celery, mushrooms and broccoli. Bring to a boil. Cover and simmer 5 minutes.

Stir in green peas and zucchini and cook 2 minutes. Season with salt and pepper. Garnish with parsley sprigs. Makes 4 servings.

—— GOLDEN VEGETABLE SOUP ——

12 ozs. carrots, chopped
8 ozs. rutabagas, chopped
2 small leeks, chopped
4 ozs. potatoes, diced
3-3/4 cups vegetable stock
1-1/4 cups milk
Salt and pepper to taste
1/4 cup plus 2 tablespoons whipping cream
1 tablespoon chopped fresh parsley
Additional chopped fresh parsley to garnish, if
    desired

In a large saucepan, combine all vegetables
and stock. Bring to a boil. Cover and simmer
30 minutes.

In a food processor or a blender, process mixture to a puree. Clean pan and return puree
to clean pan. Stir in milk. Reheat and season
with salt and pepper.

In a small bowl, whip cream until soft peaks
form. Fold in 1 tablespoon chopped parsley.
Top portions of soup with herb chantilly.
Garnish with additional chopped parsley, if
desired. Makes 4 to 6 servings.

— CREAM OF MUSHROOM SOUP —

1/4 cup butter
12 ozs. mushrooms, finely chopped
1/2 cup all-purpose flour
2 cups chicken stock
2/3 cup milk
1 tablespoon chopped fresh parsley
1 tablespoon lemon juice
Salt and pepper to taste
2/3 cup half and half
1/4 cup plus 1 tablespoon whipping cream
1 tablespoon finely chopped watercress
Watercress leaves to garnish

Melt butter in a large saucepan. Gently cook mushrooms in butter 5 minutes.

Stir in flour, then gradually add stock and milk. Bring to a boil, then simmer 10 minutes. Add parsley and lemon juice. Season with salt and pepper. Stir in half and half and reheat gently.

In a small bowl, whip cream until soft peaks form. Stir in chopped watercress. Top each portion of soup with watercress chantilly. Garnish with watercress leaves. Makes 4 servings.

SOUP GEORGETTE

2 tablespoons butter
1 medium-size onion, chopped
8 ozs. carrots, chopped
8 ozs. leeks, chopped
1 lb. tomatoes, peeled, coarsely chopped
3 cups chicken or vegetable stock
Small fresh rosemary sprig
Salt and pepper to taste
1/4 cup plus 2 tablespoons half and half
2 tomatoes and fresh rosemary sprigs
    to garnish

Melt butter in a large saucepan. Cook onion, carrots and leeks in butter 5 minutes. Stir in chopped tomatoes and cook 5 minutes.

Add stock and rosemary and bring to a boil. Cover and simmer 35 minutes. Remove rosemary. In a food processor fitted with a metal blade or a blender, process mixture to a puree. Clean pan and return puree to clean pan. Season with salt and pepper and stir in half and half.

Peel, seed and chop tomatoes. Garnish soup with chopped tomatoes and rosemary sprigs. Makes 4 servings.

——— FRENCH ONION SOUP ———

2 tablespoons butter
2 tablespoons olive oil
1 lb. onions, thinly sliced
Pinch sugar
5 cups beef stock
1 bay leaf
Salt and pepper to taste
4 thick slices French bread stick
1 teaspoon Dijon-style mustard
3/4 cup shredded Gruyère cheese (3 oz.)

Heat butter and oil in a large saucepan. Add onions and sugar.

Cook over medium heat about 20 minutes, stirring occastionally, until onions are a deep golden brown. Add stock and bay leaf and slowly bring to a boil. Simmer 25 minutes. Remove bay leaf and season with salt and pepper.

Toast bread on each side and spread with mustard. Ladle soup into 4 heat-proof bowls and top with toast. Pile cheese onto toast and broil until cheese is melted and bubbling. Serve at once. Makes 4 servings.

FRESH TOMATO & ORANGE SOUP

1 medium-size orange
1 tablespoon sunflower oil
1 small onion, chopped
1 garlic clove, crushed
1-1/2 lbs. ripe tomatoes, coarsely chopped
2 cups chicken stock
1 teaspoon sugar
1 teaspoon chopped fresh basil leaves
Salt and pepper to taste
1/4 cup whipping cream, whipped, to garnish

Using a potato peeler, cut 4 strips of peel from orange and reserve for garnish. Grate remaining peel and squeeze juice from orange.

Heat oil in a large saucepan. Cook onion and garlic in oil over low heat 5 minutes. Add grated orange peel and tomatoes and cook over medium heat 5 minutes or until tomatoes are soft. Stir in stock and add sugar and basil. Cover and simmer 15 minutes.

Meanwhile, cut reserved orange peel in thin strips. Drop in a pan of simmering water 3 minutes. Drain and spread on a paper towel. In a food processor or a blender, process soup mixture to a puree. Press puree through a sieve set over a bowl. Clean pan and return puree to clean pan. Season with salt and pepper. Stir in orange juice and reheat gently. Garnish soup with whipped cream and orange peel strips. Makes 4 servings.

FLORENTINE SOUP

1-1/2 lbs. fresh spinach
1/4 cup butter
1 shallot, chopped
1/4 cup all-purpose flour
2-1/2 cups chicken or vegetable stock
Salt and pepper to taste
1/4 teaspoon grated nutmeg
2-1/2 cups milk
3 tablespoons whipping cream
1/4 cup whipping cream and 2 very small eggs,
**   hard cooked, sliced, to garnish**

Pick over spinach, discarding stalks, and wash thoroughly.

Cook spinach in a large saucepan over medium heat until tender. Pour spinach into a colander set over a bowl and press out as much water as possible. Melt butter in a large saucepan. Cook shallot in butter until soft. Blend in flour and cook 1 minute. Add spinach and stock and simmer 15 minutes. Season with salt and pepper. Add nutmeg.

In a food processor fitted with a metal blade or a blender, process soup mixture to a puree. Clean pan and return puree to clean pan. Add milk and reheat gently. Just before serving, stir in 3 tablespoons whipping cream. To serve, swirl 1 tablespoon of whipping cream on each portion of soup and garnish with hard-cooked egg slices. Makes 4 servings.

HOT & SOUR SOUP

5 cups chicken stock
3 tablespoons rice vinegar
1 tablespoon dry sherry
2 teaspoons soy sauce
1 small garlic clove, finely chopped
1/2 teaspoon finely chopped gingerroot
5 dried Chinese mushrooms, soaked in hot
    water 20 minutes
1 carrot, cut in thin strips
1 (3-oz.) can bamboo shoots, rinsed, cut in thin
    strips
1/2 teaspoon hot-pepper sauce or chili sauce
2 tablespoons cornstarch
3 tablespoons water
4 ozs. tofu, cut in strips
2 green onions, shredded

Bring stock to a boil in a large saucepan. Stir
vinegar, sherry, soy sauce, garlic and gingerroot into stock. Remove stems from mushrooms and slice mushrooms. Add mushrooms, carrot, bamboo shoots and hot-
pepper sauce to soup mixture. Bring to a boil,
then simmer 10 minutes.

In a small bowl, blend cornstarch and water.
Stir cornstarch and water and tofu into soup.
Simmer 2 minutes or until thickened. Sprin-
kle with green onions. Makes 6 servings.

CREAMY CELERY & ONION SOUP

1 medium-size head celery
2 medium-size onions
1/4 cup butter
1 tablespoon all-purpose flour
3 cups milk
1 bay leaf
1/4 cup crème fraiche
Salt and pepper to taste

Cut 1 stalk of celery in thin strips. Place in a bowl of iced water and set aside. Reserve several celery leaves for garnish. Reserve 1/4 of 1 onion. Chop remaining onion and remaining celery.

Melt butter in a large saucepan. Cook chopped onion and celery in butter 5 minutes. Stir in flour, then gradually blend in milk. Add bay leaf, cover and simmer 20 minutes.

Cool soup slightly. Remove bay leaf. In a food processor fitted with a metal blade or a blender, process soup mixture to a puree. Clean pan and return puree to clean pan. Stir in crème fraiche. Season with salt and pepper, then reheat. Chop reserved onion and stir into soup. Drain celery curls. Garnish soup with celery curls and reserved celery leaves. Makes 4 to 6 servings.

BORSCHT

1 onion
2 large carrots
2 stalks celery
1 lb. fresh beets
6 cups strong beef stock
2 garlic cloves
1 tablespoon light-brown sugar
2 tablespoons red wine vinegar
1 bay leaf
1 teaspoon caraway seeds
Salt and pepper to taste
1 cup shredded white cabbage
8 ozs. red potatoes, boiled, peeled, diced
2/3 cup sour cream
2 tablespoons chopped fresh parsley

Julienne onion, carrots, celery, and beets in matchstick strips. Bring stock to a boil in a large saucepan. Add vegetables, garlic, brown sugar, vinegar, bay leaf and caraway seeds to stock. Season with salt and bring to a boil. Simmer 20 minutes.

Stir in cabbage and cook 20 minutes or until all vegetables are tender. Season with pepper and again with salt, if necessary. Ladle soup into warm serving bowls. Top with diced potato, sour cream and sprinkle with chopped parsley. Makes 6 servings.

–RICH COUNTRY CHICKEN SOUP–

3 tablespoons butter
4 ozs. button mushrooms, chopped
1/3 cup all-purpose flour
2-1/2 cups strong chicken stock
2-1/2 cups milk
12 ozs. cooked chicken, diced
2 egg yolks
2/3 cup half and half
Salt and pepper to taste

Watercress Dumplings:
1 cup self-rising flour
1/2 teaspoon salt
Pinch mixed dried leaf herbs
2 ozs. shredded suet
1 bunch watercress, trimmed, finely chopped
1 small egg, beaten
1 tablespoon water
Chicken stock for cooking dumplings

Melt butter in a large saucepan. Gently cook mushrooms 4 to 5 minutes. Stir in flour, then gradually add stock and milk. Bring to a boil, stirring constantly. Cover and simmer 15 minutes. Meanwhile, to prepare dumplings, sift flour into a medium-size bowl. Mix in salt, herbs, suet and watercress. Add egg and water and mix to a dough. Roll dough in 24 balls. In a large saucepan, bring stock to a boil. Drop dumplings into stock, cover and simmer 10 minutes.

Remove soup from heat and stir in chicken. In a small bowl, beat egg yolks and half and half. Ladle in a small amount of soup into half and half mixture and mix quickly. Pour back into soup and heat gently without boiling until thick. Season with salt and pepper. Using a slotted spoon, remove dumplings from stock and add to soup to serve. Makes 6 servings.

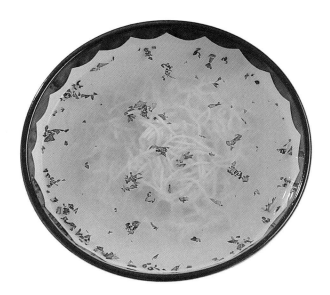

——— CHICKEN NOODLE SOUP ———

1 chicken carcass, raw or cooked, with giblets
    but not liver
1 small onion, sliced
1 large carrot, sliced
1 stalk celery, chopped
2 to 3 fresh parsley sprigs
1 teaspoon salt
6 black peppercorns
2 ozs. fine vermicelli
1 tablespoon finely chopped fresh parsley

To prepare stock, in a large deep saucepan, cover carcass with cold water and bring to a boil.

Skim off any scum that rises to surface. Add onion, carrot, celery and parsley sprigs and simmer gently 2-1/2 to 3 hours. Strain and cool carcass and stock. Refrigerate overnight. Remove any fat from surface of carcass. Measure 3-3/4 cups of stock into a large saucepan and reheat. Add salt and peppercorns.

Crumble vermicelli into a pan of boiling salted water. Simmer 4 to 5 minutes. Drain and rinse. Place drained vermicelli in a soup tureen and cover with hot soup. Sprinkle with parsley. Makes 4 servings.

SCOTCH BROTH

2 lbs. neck of lamb, cut in pieces
6 cups light stock
1/4 cup pearl barley
Salt and pepper to taste
1 large onion, chopped
2 leeks, trimmed, chopped
2 stalks celery, chopped
1 small turnip, diced
1 large carrot, sliced
Bouquet garni

In a large saucepan, combine lamb and stock. Bring slowly to a boil and skim off any scum that rises to surface.

Add barley and season with salt and pepper. Cover and simmer 2 hours. Remove meat from lamb bones. Discard fat and return meat to stock.

Add remaining ingredients to stock and bring back to a simmer. Cook 30 minutes or until vegetables are tender. Discard bouquet garni. Season again with salt and pepper, if necessary. Makes 6 servings.

MULLIGATAWNY

1 lb. boneless beef stew meat, cut in pieces
7-1/2 cups water
1 (2-inch) piece gingerroot, peeled
2 bay leaves
1 medium-size onion, chopped
1 teaspoon turmeric
1/2 teaspoon chili powder
2 teaspoons coriander seeds, crushed
2 teaspoons cumin seeds, crushed
8 black peppercorns, crushed
1 small cooking apple, peeled, cored, chopped
1 carrot, sliced
2 tablespoons red lentils
2 garlic cloves, chopped
Salt to taste
1 tablespoon lemon juice

Garlic Croutons:
2 thick slices bread
1/4 cup plus 2 tablespoons vegetable oil
3 garlic cloves, crushed

In a large saucepan, cover beef with water. Bring to a boil. Skim surface and add remaining ingredients except lemon juice. Simmer very gently 2-1/2 to 3 hours or until beef is tender. Meanwhile, to prepare croutons, cut off crusts from bread and dice bread. Heat oil in a medium-size skillet. Fry diced bread and garlic, turning bread constantly until crisp and golden. Remove with a slotted spoon and drain on a paper towel.

Remove beef and set aside. Pour stock through a sieve set over a bowl, rubbing vegetables through. Discard pulp. Cool, then refrigerate meat and stock until chilled. Remove solidified fat from surface of soup. Pour into a pan and reheat. Cut beef in small pieces. Add beef and lemon juice to soup and season again with salt, if necessary. Simmer 5 minutes. Garnish soup with croutons. Makes 4 to 6 servings.

COCK-A-LEEKIE

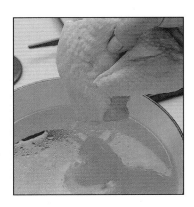

2 large chicken quarters
5 cups chicken stock
Bouquet garni
1 lb. leeks
12 prunes, soaked in water 1 hour
Salt and pepper to taste
Leek stems to garnish

Oaty Dumplings:
3/4 cup regular oats
1 cup whole-wheat bread crumbs
1 tablespoon chopped fresh herbs
Salt and pepper to taste
1/4 cup margarine, softened
2 to 3 tablespoons cold water

In a large saucepan, drop chicken into stock and add bouquet garni.

Bring to a boil, then simmer 30 minutes. Remove chicken from stock and cool. Remove bouquet garni and skim off any fat from surface of soup. Trim coarse leaves from leeks, then cut lengthwise. Wash thoroughly and cut in 1-inch pieces. Add leeks and prunes to soup. Simmer 25 minutes. Cut chicken in small pieces and add to soup. Season with salt and pepper.

To prepare dumplings, combine oats and bread crumbs in a medium-size bowl. Stir in herbs. Season with salt and pepper. Cut in margarine. Add cold water and mix to a dough. Divide in small balls and drop into soup. Cover and simmer 15 minutes. Garnish with leek stems. Makes 6 servings.

DEVILED TURKEY SOUP

1 tablespoon vegetable oil
1 medium-size onion, chopped
2 teaspoons curry powder
1/2 teaspoon dry mustard powder
12 oz. potatoes, diced
3-3/4 cups chicken stock
2 teaspoons Worcestershire sauce
6 oz. cooked turkey, diced
Salt and pepper to taste

Lemon Dumplings:
1 cup self-rising whole-wheat flour
Pinch salt
1/4 cup sunflower margarine
Grated peel and juice 1/2 lemon

Heat oil in a large saucepan. Gently cook onion in oil until soft. Stir in curry and dry mustard and cook 1 minute. Stir in potatoes and stock. Bring to a boil and simmer 30 minutes. Add Worcestershire sauce and turkey. Season with salt and pepper and slowly bring back to a simmer.

To prepare dumplings, place flour and salt in a medium-size bowl. Cut in margarine. Add lemon peel and juice and mix to a soft dough. Roll in small balls and drop into soup. Cover and cook 5 minutes or until balls are about double in size. Ladle into bowls and serve at once. Makes 4 servings.

———— GERMAN SAUSAGE SOUP ————

1 large potato, diced
1 large onion, sliced
3 stalks celery, chopped
1 (14-oz.) can chopped tomatoes
3-3/4 cups beef or ham stock
1/2 teaspoon caraway seeds
1 (8-oz.) can red kidney beans, drained
1 cup shredded cabbage
4 ozs. frankfurters, thickly sliced
1 (4 oz.) piece German sausage (bierwurst or
    ham sausage), diced
Salt and pepper to taste
Toast triangles, if desired

In a large saucepan, combine potato, onion, celery, tomatoes with juice, stock and caraway seeds.

Bring to a boil and simmer 20 minutes. Add drained beans and cabbage and simmer 20 minutes.

Stir in frankfurters and diced sausage. Season with salt and pepper and cook until heated through. Serve with toast triangles, if desired. Makes 4 to 6 servings.

— OXTAIL SOUP —

1 oxtail, cut in pieces
3 tablespoons vegetable oil
2 stalks celery, chopped
2 carrots, chopped
2 small onions, sliced
6 cups water
2/3 cup red wine
Bouquet garni
6 black peppercorns, slightly crushed
1/2 teaspoon dried leaf thyme
4 whole cloves
Salt and pepper to taste
1/4 teaspoon cayenne pepper
1 tablespoon plus 1 teaspoon arrowroot

Parsley Dumplings:
1 recipe Watercress dumplings, page 84
    (substitute 2 tablespoons chopped fresh
    parsley for watercress)

Wash oxtail and trim off any fat. Heat oil in a large saucepan. Add oxtail and fry until brown. Remove oxtail and cook vegetables in oil until they begin to brown. Add oxtail, water, wine, bouquet garni, peppercorns, thyme and cloves. Season with salt and pepper. Bring to a boil, skimming off any scum. Cover and simmer over very low heat 3 hours. Remove oxtail and cool. Remove meat from bones, discarding gristle. Strain soups through a sieve set over a bowl. Add oxtail meat to stock.

Prepare dumplings. Begin to reheat soup. In a small bowl, blend arrowroot with a small amount of water. Stir arrowroot and cayenne pepper into soup. Season again with salt and pepper, if necessary. When soup simmers, drop in dumplings. Cover and cook 20 minutes or until dumplings are done. Makes 6 servings.

BEEF & PASTA SOUP

6 ozs. capellini (very fine spaghetti)

Beef Stock:
1 lb. boneless beef stew meat, cut in pieces
1 lb. marrow bones or knuckle of veal
7-1/2 cups water
1 medium-size onion, sliced
1 large carrot, sliced
Bouquet garni
1 teaspoon salt
5 peppercorns
1 bay leaf

Parmesan Balls:
1/4 cup freshly grated Parmesan cheese
2 egg yolks

Preheat oven to 425F (220C). In a large roasting pan, bake meat and bones in preheated oven 15 minutes or until brown. Turn meat and bones over and bake another 10 minutes. Transfer meat to a large saucepan. Add water and bring to a boil. Skim off scum which rises to surface. When only white foam is left, add onion, carrot, bouquet garni, salt, peppercorns and bay leaf. Simmer very gently 3 hours. This should yield 5 cups stock.

Strain stock, cool and refrigerate overnight. Next day, remove fat from surface of stock and return to a large saucepan. Reheat stock, seasoning again with salt and pepper, if necessary. When soup simmers, break up pasta and drop into soup. Cook 6 minutes. Meanwhile, to prepare Parmesan balls, mix cheese and egg yolks in a small bowl. Drop 1/2 teaspoonfuls of mixture over surface of soup. Cook about 4 minutes or until balls and pasta are done. Serve at once. Makes 6 servings.

GOULASH SOUP

2 tablespoons vegetable oil
1 lb. lean beef stew meat, cut in 1/4-inch cubes
1 large onion, thinly sliced
1 garlic clove, crushed
1/2 teaspoon ground cumin
2 teaspoons paprika
1 tablespoon all-purpose flour
5 cups beef stock
1 large potato
1 (14-oz.) can tomatoes, chopped, with juice
Salt and pepper to taste
Sour cream and paprika to garnish

Heat oil in a large saucepan and add beef and onion.

Cook over medium heat 4 minutes or until beef is brown and onion is soft. Stir in garlic, cumin, paprika and flour and cook 1 minute. Gradually add stock. Bring to a boil, then simmer 2 hours.

Dice potatoes. Add potatoes and tomatoes with juice to soup. Season with salt and pepper. Cook 30 minutes or until potatoes are tender. Garnish soup with sour cream and sprinkle with paprika. Makes 6 servings.

HARIRA

2 tablespoons vegetables oil
12 ozs. boneless lean lamb, cut in small cubes
1 medium-size onion, sliced
2 teaspoons ground coriander
1/2 teaspoon ground turmeric
1/2 teaspoon cayenne pepper
1/2 teaspoon ground ginger
1/2 teaspoon ground cumin
8 ozs. tomatoes, peeled, chopped
1 garlic clove, crushed
2-1/2 cups water
1 (14-oz.) can garbanzo beans, drained
Salt and pepper to taste
Juice 2 limes or 1 lemon
1 tablespoon chopped fresh cilantro
1/4 teaspoon ground cinnamon to garnish

Heat oil in a large saucepan. Fry lamb in oil quickly until evenly browned all over. Reduce heat and add onion. Cook 5 minutes, stirring constantly. Stir in all spices. Cook 1 minute and add tomatoes, garlic and water.

In a small bowl, mash 3/4 of garbanzo beans. Add mashed and whole beans to soup. Season with salt and pepper. Bring to a boil and simmer 40 minutes or until lamb is tender. Just before serving, stir in lime juice and cilantro and simmer 2 minutes. Sprinkle soup with cinnamon. Makes 4 to 6 servings.

—— PHEASANT & LENTIL SOUP ——

1 small pheasant, cleaned
7-1/2 cups water
1 onion, thickly sliced
1 large carrot, thickly sliced
2 stalks celery, chopped
1 bay leaf
8 peppercorns
Fresh thyme sprig
2/3 cup brown lentils
2 small leeks, trimmed, chopped
Salt and pepper to taste

In a large saucepan, cover pheasant with water. Bring slowly to a boil and skim off scum from surface.

Add onion, carrot, celery, bay leaf, peppercorns and thyme sprig. Cover and simmer 45 minutes. Remove pheasant and cool. Remove breast meat. Return carcass to stock and cook 2 hours. Strain stock through a sieve set over a bowl. Cool and refrigerate stock and reserved breast meat and best bits of leg meat overnight. Next day, remove layer of fat from soup. Measure stock and return to pan. Bring to a boil. Reduce stock to 6 cups by simmering, adding water if necessary.

Add lentils and leeks to stock. Cover and simmer 45 minutes or until lentils are tender. Meanwhile, dice reserved meat and add to soup. Season with salt and pepper and simmer a few minutes until heated through. Makes 6 servings.

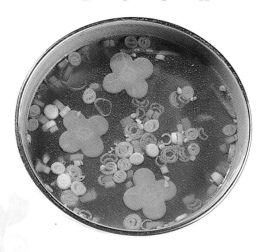

—— ORIENTAL CHICKEN SOUP ——

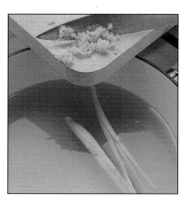

Chicken Consommé:
4 ozs. minced veal
1 carrot, finely chopped
1 stalk celery, finely chopped
1 leek, trimmed, finely sliced
1 thyme sprig
1 bay leaf
7-1/2 cups chicken stock
Salt and pepper to taste
2 egg whites

Soup:
1 garlic clove, finely chopped
1 stalk lemon grass, cut in half lengthwise
Carrot flowers
2 green onions, sliced
2 ozs. cooked chicken breast, shredded
2 ozs. Chinese snow peas, trimmed, cut in
    strips

To prepare consommé, combine veal, vegetables, herbs and stock in a large saucepan. Season with salt and pepper and begin to heat. Whisk egg whites in a small bowl and pour into stock mixture, whisking continually until a thick froth begins to form. When stock mixture reaches boiling point, stop whisking and lower heat to maintain a very slow simmer. Do not allow mixture to boil. Cook consommé 1 hour.

Line a large sieve or colander with muslin and set over a bowl. Draw scum back from surface of consommé sufficiently to ladle liquid. Ladle clarified stock into muslin-lined sieve. Place a paper towel over surface to absorb any fat. Measure 3-3/4 cups consommé into a large saucepan. Add garlic and lemon grass and simmer 15 minutes. Meanwhile, blanch carrot flowers in boiling salted water 2 minutes. Remove lemon grass and add green onions, chicken and snow peas and simmer 2 minutes. Add carrot flowers just before serving. Makes 4 servings.

CHICKEN LIVER SOUP

4 ozs. chicken livers
2 tablespoons butter
1 shallot, finely chopped
1/4 cup all-purpose flour
2-1/2 cups chicken stock
Salt and pepper to taste
3 tablespoons dry sherry

Egg Balls:
2 hard-cooked eggs
1 egg yolk
1 teaspoon chopped fresh parsley
1/2 cup fresh bread crumbs
Salt and pepper to taste
2 tablespoons ground almonds

Clean chicken livers. Melt butter in a large saucepan. Gently cook shallot in butter until soft. Add livers and cook 1 minute. Stir in flour and cook 1 minute, then gradually add stock. Season with salt and pepper and simmer 3 to 4 minutes. Pour mixture through a sieve set over a bowl. Clean pan and return sieved mixture to clean pan. Add sherry and season again, if necessary.

To prepare egg balls, press hard-cooked eggs through a sieve set over a bowl. Mix with remaining ingredients to make a stiff paste. With floured hands, roll in tiny balls. Drop balls into a pan of simmering salted water and cook 5 minutes. Reheat soup without boiling. Remove egg balls with a slotted spoon and drop into soup. Serve immediately with toast triangles, if desired. Makes 4 servings.

ITALIAN MEATBALL SOUP

Meatballs:
6 ozs. very lean ground beef
1 small egg
1 teaspoon finely chopped onion
1 tablespoon fresh bread crumbs
2 teaspoons chopped fresh parsley
Salt and pepper to taste
Pinch grated nutmeg

Soup:
3-3/4 cups beef consommé, page 108
1 tablespoon butter
1 large carrot, julienned in thin matchstick
    strips
1 leek, shredded
1 small turnip, julienned in thin matchstick
    strips
Salt and pepper to taste

To prepare meatballs, in a medium-size bowl, combine all meatball ingredients. With dampened hands, roll ground beef in 16 small walnut-size balls. Bring a pan of water to a boil. Lower heat to simmer and drop in meatballs. Gently cook 10 minutes. Remove meatballs with a slotted spoon and set aside.

In a large saucepan, combine 2/3 cup of consommé, butter and vegetables. Cover and cook over medium heat 5 minutes. Add remaining consommé and meatballs. Bring to a boil and simmer 2 to 3 minutes or until meatballs are reheated. Season with salt and pepper. Makes 4 servings.

— CHICKEN & KNEIDLACH SOUP —

1 large chicken breast
1 medium-size onion, chopped
1 large carrot, chopped
5 cups chicken stock
Chervil leaves to garnish

Kneidlach (dumplings):
2 tablespoons vegetable oil
1 small onion, finely chopped
1/2 cup medium matzah meal
1 tablespoon ground almonds
1 egg, beaten
1/2 cup boiling water
Salt and pepper to taste

In a large saucepan, combine chicken, onion, carrots and stock. Season with salt and pepper and bring to a boil. Cover and simmer 1 hour. Meanwhile, to prepare kneidlach, heat oil in a small skillet. Saute onion in oil until soft. Strain oil into a bowl and discard onion. Stir in matzah meal, ground almonds, egg and boiling water. Season with salt and pepper. Mix well to make a soft dough. Cover and refrigerate 30 minutes.

Remove chicken from stock. Strain stock into another large saucepan. Cut chicken in small pieces and return to soup. To cook kneidlach, roll dough in 12 small balls with damp hands. Bring a pan of water to simmering and drop balls into water. Cover and simmer 6 to 8 minutes or until balls are double in size. Remove balls with a slotted spoon and drop into soup. Garnish soup with chervil leaves. Makes 6 servings.

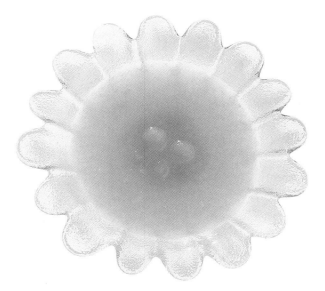

ICED MELON SOUP

1 (1-1/2-lb.) honeydew melon
1 (1-1/2 lb.) cantaloupe
2-1/2 cups water
1 small piece gingerroot, peeled
1/2 cup sugar
1 cup dry white wine

Cut melons in half and discard seeds. Scoop out a few small balls from honeydew melon and set aside. Scoop remaining flesh from melons, keeping 2 varieties separate.

In a medium-size saucepan, combine water, gingerroot and sugar. Simmer 5 minutes. Cool and remove gingerroot. In a food processor fitted with a metal blade, process honeydew melon, 1/2 of cooled syrup and 1/2 of wine until blended. Pour into a bowl. Process cantaloupe and remaining syrup and wine until blended.

Chill both bowls of soup at least 1 hour. To serve, pour honeydew melon soup into individual bowls. Pour cantaloupe soup into middle of honeydew melon soup. Garnish with reserved melon balls. Makes 4 to 6 servings.

—— SUMMER TOMATO BISQUE ——

2 lbs. ripe tomatoes, chopped
3 green onions, chopped
1/2 red bell pepper, seeded, chopped
2 garlic cloves, crushed
2 cups vegetable stock
1 teaspoon sugar
2 tablespoons chopped fresh basil
1/4 cup crème fraiche or plain yogurt
Salt and pepper to taste
1 avocado and snipped chives to garnish

In a large saucepan, combine tomatoes, green onions, bell pepper, garlic, stock and sugar. Bring to a boil, then simmer 15 minutes. Remove from heat and cool.

In a food processor fitted with a metal blade or a blender, process mixture to a puree. Press puree through a sieve set over a bowl. Cover and refrigerate 2 hours to chill. Stir in basil and crème fraiche. Season with salt and pepper.

Cut avocado in half. Remove seed, peel and slice. Ladle soup into individual bowls. Arrange avocado slices on soup and sprinkle with snipped chives. Makes 6 servings.

SNOW PEA SOUP

2 tablespoons butter
5 green onions, chopped
12 ozs. Chinese snow peas, trimmed
2-1/2 cups chicken stock
1/2 small head lettuce, shredded
1 teaspoon sugar
Salt and pepper to taste
1 tablespoon chopped fresh mint
2/3 cup crème fraiche
2 slices bread
Oil for frying

Melt butter in a large saucepan. Gently cook green onions in butter 3 to 4 minutes.

Reserve 6 snow peas for garnish and chop remaining. Add chopped snow peas, stock, lettuce and sugar to green onions. Simmer 5 minutes. In a food processor fitted with a metal blade or a blender, process mixture to a puree. Press puree through a sieve set over a bowl. Clean pan and return puree to clean pan. Season with salt and pepper. Stir in mint and crème fraiche and reheat gently. Do not allow to boil. Do not reheat too long or soup will loose its fresh color.

Shred 6 reserved snow peas. Blanch 30 seconds in boiling salted water and drain. To prepare croutons, cut bread in fancy shapes and fry in oil until crisp and golden. Drain on paper towels. Garnish soup with shredded snow peas and croutons. Makes 4 servings.

PUMPKIN SOUP

1 (3-lb.) pumpkin
2 tablespoons butter
1 medium-size onion, chopped
2-1/2 cups chicken stock
1 teaspoon light-brown sugar
2/3 cup half and half
1/4 teaspoon paprika
Good pinch grated nutmeg
Salt and pepper to taste

Paprika Niblets:
3 slices bread
Oil for frying
Paprika

Discard pumpkin seeds and stringy bits.

Cut out pumpkin flesh and dice. Melt butter in a large saucepan. Cook onion in butter until soft. Add diced pumpkin, stock and brown sugar. Bring to a boil, then simmer 30 minutes. In a food processor fitted with a metal blade or a blender, process mixture to a puree. Clean pan and return puree to clean pan. Stir in half and half, paprika and nutmeg. Season with salt and pepper. Reheat slowly.

Meanwhile, cut out attractive shapes from bread or make rings using 2 cutters, 1 slightly larger than other. Heat 1/4-inch of oil in a medium-size skillet and fry bread until golden. Drain on paper towels, then dust with paprika. Garnish soup with fried bread. Makes 6 servings.

CONSOMMÉ MADRILENE

5 cups chicken stock
1 lb. tomatoes, chopped
4 stalks celery, finely chopped
1 (2-oz.) can chopped pimientos
1 lemon peel strip
2 egg whites
2 tablespoons dry sherry
2 ozs. pimientos, diced
1 tomato, peeled, diced
Salt and pepper to taste

Soup Nuts:
2 teaspoons vegetable oil
1/2 teaspoon salt
1 egg
3/4 cup all-purpose flour
Additional oil for frying

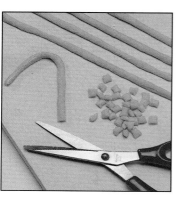

To prepare consommé, combine stock, tomatoes, celery, pimientos and lemon peel in a large saucepan. Whisk in egg whites. Bring to a boil, stirring constantly, then simmer very slowly 1 hour. To prepare Soup Nuts, place 2 tablespoons oil, salt and egg into a food processor fitted with a metal blade. Add flour and process to a smooth dough. Roll out dough in thin rolls about 1/4 inch thick and let dry 10 minutes. With scissors, snip rolls in 1/4-inch pieces and let dry 30 minutes.

Heat oil in a deep medium-size skillet. Fry dough pieces until crisp and golden. Drain on paper towels. Strain consommé through a muslin-lined sieve set over a bowl. Clean pan and return strained consommé to clean pan. Stir in sherry, pimientos and tomato. Season with salt and pepper and reheat. Serve soup with Soup Nuts. Makes 4 to 6 servings.

— TARRAGON & TOMATO SOUP —

3 ozs. sorrel leaves
1 lb. ripe tomatoes
2 tablespoons olive oil
1 small onion, chopped
2 cups vegetable stock
2/3 cup dry white wine
2 egg yolks
2/3 cup half and half
Salt and pepper to taste
1 tablespoon chopped fresh tarragon
Additional half and half and fresh tarragon
  sprigs to garnish

Trim stalks from sorrel and chop tomatoes. Heat oil in a large saucepan. Cook onion in oil until soft.

Add sorrel leaves and tomatoes and cook over very low heat 15 minutes. Stir in stock and wine and cook 10 minutes. Press mixture through a sieve set over a bowl. Clean pan and return puree to clean pan.

In a small bowl, beat egg yolks and half and half. Mix a small amount of puree into egg yolk mixture. Pour back into puree and re-heat to thicken. Season with salt and pepper and stir in chopped tarragon. Garnish with half and half and tarragon sprigs. Makes 4 to 6 servings.

SAFFRON SOUP WITH QUENELLES

1 medium-size onion, chopped
8 ozs. potatoes, chopped
8 ozs. white fish fillets, skinned, chopped
3-3/4 cups fish stock
1/4 teaspoon powdered saffron
Salt and pepper to taste
2/3 cup half and half
Fresh dill sprigs to garnish

Trout Quenelles:
8 ozs. pink trout fillets, skinned
1 teaspoon anchovy essence
1 cup day-old white bread crumbs
2 eggs, separated

In a large saucepan, combine onion, potatoes, fish and stock. Gently simmer 25 minutes or until potatoes are tender. Meanwhile, to prepare Trout Quenelles, process trout, anchovy essence, bread crumbs and egg yolks in a food processor fitted with metal blade or a blender until smooth. Spoon into a bowl and refrigerate until chilled. In food processor fitted with metal blade or a blender, process stock mixture to a puree. Press through a sieve set over a bowl. Clean pan and return puree to clean pan. Stir in saffron and half and half. Reheat very gently. Season with salt and pepper.

In a small bowl, whisk egg whites until stiff. Fold into trout mixture. Bring a pan of salted water or fish stock to a boil, then reduce to a simmer. Drop heaping teaspoonfuls of trout mixture into hot water and cook 2 to 3 minutes. When done, they will float to surface. Remove with a slotted spoon and place on top of reheated soup. Garnish soup with dill sprigs. Makes 6 servings.

—————— BOUILLABAISSE ——————

2 lbs. mixed fish (monkfish, cod, squid, mullet)
1 lb. shellfish (shrimp, mussels, scallops)
6 cups water
1 medium-size onion, sliced
1 carrot, sliced
1 stalk celery, chopped
1 bay leaf
Salt and pepper to taste
2 tablespoons olive oil
2 garlic cloves, finely chopped
2 small leeks, trimmed, finely chopped
4 tomatoes, peeled, chopped
Fresh fennel sprigs
3 orange peel strips
Good pinch saffron threads
1 fresh thyme sprig
Salt and pepper to taste
French bread, sliced, toasted
1 recipe Rouille, page 32

Clean and prepare fish, removing skin and bones. Reserve fish trimmings. Cut fish in chunks. Shellfish can be left unpeeled. Remove heads, if desired. In a large saucepan, combine fish trimmings and bones, water, onion, carrot, celery and bay leaf. Bring to a boil. Season with salt and pepper. Remove any scum which rises to surface and simmer 30 minutes. Strain stock into a large bowl, discarding bones and vegetables.

Clean saucepan. Heat oil in clean pan. Cook garlic and leeks over low heat 5 minutes. Add tomatoes and cook 5 minutes. Pour in stock and bring to a boil. Stir in fennel, orange peel, saffron and thyme. When mixture boils, reduce heat and add firmer white fish and simmer 8 minutes. Add shellfish and cook 5 minutes. Season with salt and pepper. Spread toast with Rouille and serve with soup. Makes 6 servings.

—— SURPRISE BEEF CONSOMMÉ ——

5 cups beef stock
8 ozs. lean ground beef
1 small onion, chopped
1 carrot, chopped
2 egg whites
Salt to taste
2 teaspoons Madeira wine or dry sherry
1 small truffle
12 ozs. puff pastry, thawed if frozen
1 egg, beaten

Remove any fat from stock. In a large saucepan, combine stock, ground beef and vegetables.

Whisk in egg whites. Bring slowly to a boil, whisking constantly. A thick gray scum will rise to surface. Reduce heat and simmer very gently, uncovered, 1 hour. Draw back scum and ladle clarified stock into a muslin-lined sieve set over a bowl. Consommé should be clear and sparkling. Season with salt and stir in wine. Ladle consommé into 6 individual ovenproof bowls. Cut truffle in small cubes and divide between bowls.

Preheat oven to 400F (205C). Roll out pastry and cut out 6 lids large enough to cover bowls, allowing enough to slightly overlap edge so pastry does not fall into soup. Brush top of pastry with beaten egg. Place bowls on a baking sheet. Bake in preheated oven 15 minutes or until pastry is risen and golden. Serve immediately. Makes 6 servings.

OYSTER & LEEK SOUP

18 medium-size oysters, in shell
2 tablespoons butter
3 medium-size leeks, trimmed, thinly sliced
1 shallot, finely chopped
1/2 cup dry white wine
2 cups light fish stock
1 cup half and half
Salt and pepper to taste
4 (2-inch) fried bread rounds to garnish

Holding oysters over a bowl to catch juices, insert point of an oyster knife or a sharp short-bladed vegetable knife at hinge of oyster shells and twist open. Remove oysters and put into bowl.

Melt butter in a large saucepan. Gently cook leeks in butter 5 minutes or until leeks begin to soften. Remove with a slotted spoon and set aside. Cook shallot in butter until soft. Stir in wine and simmer, uncovered, 5 minutes. Add stock and simmer 5 minutes.

Meanwhile, in a food processor fitted with a metal blade or a blender, process 1/2 of oysters with their juice until coarsely chopped. Cut remaining oysters in half. Stir chopped and halved oysters, 3/4 of leeks and half and half into stock mixture. Season with salt and pepper. Reheat very slowly. Do not allow to boil. Maintain a heat below simmering 3 to 4 minutes or until oysters are just cooked. Reheat remaining leeks in a small skillet. Spoon leeks onto fried bread rounds. Float bread rings on soup. Makes 4 servings.

LOBSTER BISQUE

1 (1-1/2 lb.) female lobster
1/3 cup butter
1 small onion, finely chopped
1 carrot, finely chopped
2 stalks celery, finely chopped
2 tablespoons brandy
2/3 cup dry white wine
6 cups fish stock
3 lemon peel strips
3 tablespoons white long-grain rice
Salt and pepper to taste
2 slices toast to garnish

Remove eggs from lobster and reserve.

Remove claws and split tail in half. Remove meat from body, discarding intestinal tube. Crack claws and remove meat. Remove stomach sac and gills from head part. Scoop out green "cream" and reserve. Crush claw shells. In a food processor fitted with metal blade or a blender, process softer body shell and feelers until broken up. Melt 3/4 of butter in a large saucepan. Gently cook vegetables 10 minutes. Stir in broken claw and shells. Pour over brandy and ignite. When flames subside, stir in wine, 3/4 of stock and lemon peel. Bring to a boil, cover and simmer 25 minutes. Cook rice in remaining stock.

Reserve a small amount of lobster meat. In food processor fitted with metal blade or blender, process "cream" and rice. Strain soup into a bowl. Add a small amount of soup to mixture in food processor and process again; whisk into soup. Season and gently reheat. Cut 6 small rounds from toast. Heat remaining butter. Stir in reserved eggs and warm through. Top toast with eggs. Stir remaining eggs and reserved lobster meat into soup. Place toast on soup. Makes 6 servings.

—— CREAM OF BROCCOLI SOUP ——

2 tablespoons butter
2 shallots, finely chopped
1 lb. broccoli flowerets, chopped
1 large potato, diced
1 garlic clove, crushed
2 cups vegetable stock
2 cups milk
Pinch grated nutmeg
Salt and pepper to taste
2/3 cup half and half, 2 tablespoons ground
    almonds and 1/4 teaspoon powdered saffron
    to garnish

Melt butter in a large saucepan. Cook shallots in butter 2 to 3 minutes or until soft. Add broccoli, potato and garlic. Cover and cook gently 5 minutes. Add stock and bring to a boil, then simmer 20 minutes or until vegetables are tender. In a food processor fitted with a metal blade or a blender, process mixture to a puree. Clean pan and return puree to clean pan. Add milk and nutmeg. Season with salt and pepper and reheat gently.

Divide half and half between 2 small bowls. Mix ground almonds into 1 bowl and saffron into other. Ladle soup into individual bowls. Garnish soup with alternate swirls of half and half mixtures. Makes 4 servings.

THAI CUCUMBER & PORK SOUP

**4 dried Chinese mushrooms, soaked 20 minutes
   in hot water**
3-3/4 cups chicken stock
6 ozs. pork tenderloin, cut in thin strips
1 tablespoon cornstarch
2 tablespoons soy sauce
2 tablespoons rice vinegar
1/2 cucumber, cut in thin strips
1-3/4 cups shredded Chinese cabbage

Remove stalks from mushrooms. Cut in thin
slices. In a large saucepan, combine
mushrooms and stock. Bring to a boil.

Place pork strips on a large plate. Sprinkle
with cornstarch and roll lightly to coat. Add
coated pork strips, soy sauce and vinegar to
stock. Simmer 5 minutes.

Stir in cucumber and Chinese cabbage and
simmer 2 minutes. Do not overcook or soup
will lose texture and flavor. Ladle soup into
serving bowls. Makes 4 to 6 servings.

RED & YELLOW BELL PEPPER SOUP

1/4 cup butter
1 large onion, chopped
2 garlic cloves, crushed
8 ozs. tomatoes, coarsely chopped
8 ozs. red bell peppers, seeded, chopped
5 cups vegetable stock
8 ozs. yellow bell peppers, seeded, chopped
Salt and pepper to taste
1 tablespoon arrowroot
Water
1 oz. blanched almonds or pine nuts
1/2 slice white bread, crust removed
1/2 cup half and half

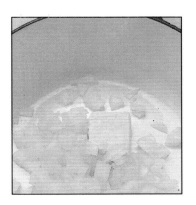

Place 1/2 of butter, 1/2 of onion and 1 garlic clove in a large saucepan.

Place remaining butter, onion and garlic in another large saucepan. Gently cook both until onion is soft. Add tomatoes, red bell peppers and 1/2 of stock to 1 pan. Add yellow bell peppers and remaining stock to other pan. Simmer both mixtures 20 minutes. In a food processor fitted with a metal blade or a blender, process 1 mixture to a puree. Press puree through a sieve set over a bowl. Clean pan and return puree to clean pan. Repeat procedure with remaining mixture. Season both purees with salt and pepper. In a small bowl, blend arrowroot with a small amount of water and stir into red bell pepper mixture. Reheat to thicken.

In food processor fitted with a metal blade or blender, process almonds, bread and half and half to a puree. Stir into yellow bell pepper puree and reheat. Pour each soup into a pitcher. Pour soups into individual bowls, pouring red bell pepper soup from 1 side and yellow bell pepper soup from opposite side. Serve at once. Makes 6 servings.

WATERCRESS CONSOMMÉ

Herb Pasta:
1 cup all-purpose flour
1 egg, beaten
1 teaspoon vegetable oil
2 teaspoons finely chopped fresh herbs
3 tablespoons water

Consommé:
3-3/4 cups beef consommé
2 small carrots, peeled, sliced, cut in flowers
12 watercress sprigs
3 tablespoons Madeira wine
Salt and pepper to taste

To prepare pasta, place flour in a medium-size bowl. Make a well in center and add egg, oil, herbs and water.

Mix until dough is soft and pliable. Turn onto a floured surface and knead until smooth. Wrap dough and let stand 30 minutes. Roll dough out thinly. Cover with a cloth and let dry 30 minutes, turning over after 15 minutes. Meanwhile, in a large saucepan, combine consommé, carrot and watercress stalks. Simmer 8 minutes.

Cut out small fancy shapes from pasta. Drop into boiling salted water and cook about 8 minutes or until tender. Remove watercress stalks from soup. Stir in watercress leaves and wine. Season with salt and pepper. Add pasta to consommé. Serve hot. Makes 4 to 6 servings.

—— ORIENTAL SCALLOP SOUP ——

8 medium-size scallops
2 teaspoons chopped gingerroot
2 tablespoons dry sherry
1 tablespoon light soy sauce
3-3/4 cups chicken stock
2 garlic cloves, thinly sliced
1/2 red bell pepper, cut in diamonds
1/2 yellow bell pepper, cut in diamonds
2 ozs. pea starch noodles, soaked 5 minutes,
    drained
Salt and pepper to taste

Rinse scallops and drain. Reserve pink corals.
Cut white part in quarters. In a medium-size
bowl, combine quartered scallops, gingerroot, sherry and soy sauce.

Stir to coat scallops with marinade and refrigerate. In a large saucepan, combine stock
and garlic. Bring to a boil. Cover and simmer
15 minutes. Add bell peppers and noodles
and cook 3 minutes or until noodles are
tender.

Stir in reserved corals and scallops with marinade. Cook about 2 minutes or until scallops
are opaque. Season with salt and pepper and
serve at once. Makes 4 servings.

– SMOKED SALMON & DILL SOUP –

2 tablespoons butter
2 shallots, finely chopped
2 tablespoons all-purpose flour
2-1/2 cups milk
1/2 fish stock cube, crumbled
1 cucumber, peeled, chopped
6 ozs. smoked salmon bits
1 tablespoon chopped fresh dill
2/3 cup half and half
Salt and pepper to taste
Lemon pieces and fresh dill sprigs to garnish

Melt butter in a large saucepan. Gently cook shallots in butter until soft. Stir in flour, then gradually add milk. Bring to a boil. Add stock cube and cucumber.

Simmer 10 minutes. Reserve several salmon bits for garnish. Chop remaining salmon bits and add to stock mixture. Cook gently 2 to 3 minutes.

In a food processor fitted with a metal blade or a blender, process soup to a puree. Clean pan and return puree to clean pan. Stir in chopped dill and half and half. Season with salt and pepper and gently reheat. Garnish with reserved salmon bits, lemon pieces and dill sprigs. Makes 4 servings.

— CREAM OF ASPARAGUS SOUP —

1-1/2 lbs. fresh thin asparagus spears
3 tablespoons butter
1 bunch green onions, trimmed, chopped
2 tablespoons all-purpose flour
3-3/4 cups light chicken stock
2 egg yolks
2/3 cup half and half
Salt and pepper to taste
Additional half and half to garnish

Wash asparagus and cut off tops. Gently simmer tops in salted water 3 to 5 minutes or until just tender. Drain and set aside. Cut off woody ends of stalks. Scrape to remove scales, then chop stalks.

Melt butter in a large saucepan. Cook chopped asparagus and green onions 5 minutes. Stir in flour, then gradually add stock. Simmer about 20 to 25 minutes or until asparagus is tender.

Cool stock mixture slightly. In a food processor fitted with a metal blade or a blender, process stock mixture to a puree. Press puree through a sieve set over a bowl. Clean pan and return puree to clean pan. Beat egg yolks in a small bowl. Whisk a small amount of puree into beaten egg yolks, then return mixture to puree. Stir in 2/3 cup half and half and gently reheat until soup has a creamy texture. Season with salt and pepper. Stir in reserved asparagus tips and heat 2 minutes. Garnish each portion of soup with a swirl of half and half. Makes 6 servings.

GAZPACHO

1 lb. ripe tomatoes, peeled, chopped
1/2 cucumber, peeled, chopped
1 green bell pepper, seeded, chopped
1 red bell pepper, seeded, chopped
1 small onion, chopped
1 garlic clove, chopped
1 cup bread crumbs
2 tablespoons olive oil
2 tablespoons red wine vinegar
2 cups tomato juice
1/2 teaspoon dried leaf marjoram
Salt and pepper to taste

Process all ingredients in a food processor fitted with a metal blade or a blender. Process in 2 batches if necessary.

Blend until smooth. Soup should be consistency of half and half. If soup is too thick, add a small amount of iced water. Spoon soup into a bowl. Cover and refrigerate about 2 hours.

When soup is well chilled, season again with salt and pepper, if necessary, and add a few ice cubes. Makes 4 to 6 servings.

Note: Gazpacho is traditionally served with a selection of garnishes passed separately. These are added to individual portions as desired. Serve chopped hard-cooked eggs, chopped cucumber, chopped onion, chopped green or black olives and diced green bell pepper in separate small bowls.

—— HARLEQUIN CONSOMMÉ ——

1 lb. very lean ground beef
1 carrot, coarsely chopped
2 leeks, coarsely chopped
1/2 large red bell pepper, chopped
1/4 cup plus 1 tablespoon tomato paste
2 egg whites
5 cups beef stock
White of 1 hard-cooked egg
1/2 red bell pepper, peeled, page 61
Green leek leaves, blanched
1 carrot
Salt and pepper to taste

To prepare consommé, combine ground beef, chopped vegetables, tomato paste, egg whites and stock. Bring to a boil, whisking constantly. Reduce to a low simmer and cook 1-1/2 hours without stirring. Meanwhile, slice hard-cooked egg white and cut in small fancy shapes with aspic cutters. Cut shapes out of bell pepper and green leek leaves. Slice carrot thinly lengthwise, discarding core. Cut shapes from carrot strips.

Strain consommé through a muslin-lined sieve set over a bowl. Clean pan and return consommé to clean pan. Season with salt and pepper. Add bell pepper, leek and carrot shapes. Cook 1 minute, then add egg white shapes. Makes 6 servings.

INDEX